MOUNTAINS OF BRITAIN

1 (overleaf) *Buttermere and Fleetwith Pike*

MOUNTAINS OF BRITAIN

EDWARD C PYATT

B T BATSFORD LTD LONDON

First published 1966

© Edward C Pyatt 1966

MADE AND PRINTED IN GREAT BRITAIN
BY WILLIAM CLOWES AND SONS LTD, LONDON AND BECCLES
FOR THE PUBLISHERS B T BATSFORD LTD
4 FITZHARDINGE STREET, PORTMAN SQUARE, LONDON W1

CONTENTS

THE ILLUSTRATIONS

THE MAPS

ACKNOWLEDGMENT

A book of this sort owes something to a great many people, not only to my family and to the various friends who have been my companions among the hills of Britain during the last 30 years, but also to the authors of innumerable books and articles on climbing, walking, caving and other outdoor topics which have formed a background to the interest of a lifetime. Climbing Club journals, and particularly those of the Climbers', Scottish Mountaineering, Fell and Rock Climbing, Irish Mountaineering, Rucksack and Yorkshire Ramblers' Clubs, are a prolific source of information; from them alone is it possible to chart the course of the development of all the various aspects of mountain lore which surround us today.

I have pleasure in acknowledging my indebtedness to the following publishers for permission to quote from the undermentioned books: Longmans, Green & Co. Ltd., for *Rock Climbing in the British Isles* (*England*) by W. P. Haskett Smith and *Rock Climbing in the British Isles* (*Wales and Ireland*) by W. P. Haskett Smith and H. C. Hart; Chapman and Hall Ltd. for *Caving* by E. A. Baker; J. M. Dent & Sons Ltd. (and W. H. Murray) for *Mountaineering in Scotland* by W. H. Murray; Eyre and Spottiswoode Ltd., for *Mountains with a Difference* by Geoffrey Winthrop Young; The National Trust for Scotland (and W. H. Murray) for *Highland Landscape* by W. H. Murray; Mr G. P. Abraham for quotations from Ashley P. Abraham in *Rock Climbing in Skye* and *Rock Climbing in North Wales*.

I am grateful also to the following for permission to quote from their writings, mostly in journal articles: J. A. Austin, J. H. B. Bell, Robin Campbell, H. R. C. Carr, I. Clough, S. de Courcy, H. Drasdo, A. B. Hargreaves, P. Kenny, Brighid MacCall, T. Patey, H. T. H. Peck, P. Ross and G. S. Sansom.

ACKNOWLEDGMENT

The works of C. W. Wall and R. L. Praeger on Ireland, and the Scottish Mountaineering Club guidebooks to Scotland have been particularly helpful.

I am indebted to the following for photographs:

G. Douglas Bolton for fig. 13
Bord Fáilte Éireann for figs. 3, 19, 20 and 22
British Travel Association for figs. 6 and 7
J. Allan Cash for fig. 9
Gamma Photography for figs. 10 and 11
Leonard and Marjorie Gayton for figs. 4, 5 and 15
Noel Habgood for figs. 24–26
D. C. Haiselden for fig. 1
Northern Ireland Tourist Board (J. Allan Cash) for fig. 23
W. A. Poucher for figs. 2, 8, 12, 17, 21, 27, 29 and 30
Kenneth Scowen for figs. 16 and 18
E. A. Shepherd for figs. 14 and 28

My wife has given tremendous help and encouragement at all stages of the project; Christopher and Gillian also made some contribution.

Edward C. Pyatt
Hampton Hill

Introduction

John Ray, writing in 1692, had this to say of mountains:

> Because they have been lookt upon by some as Warts and superfluous
> Excrescencies, of no use or benefit; nay, rather as signs and proofs that
> the present Earth is nothing else but a heap of rubbish and Ruins, I shall
> deduce and demonstrate in Particulars, the great Use, Benefit and Neces-
> sity of them . . .

Splendid sentiments! Now nearly 300 years later, though our appreci-
ation is much more diversified, the main purpose of a book on mountains, such as this one, is still to 'deduce and demonstrate in Particulars
the great Use, Benefit and Necessity of them'. This then can be our
watchword.

The dictionary makes no clear distinction between a hill and a
mountain, though we can perhaps agree with the definition of Gerard
Boate (1652), who held that hills are 'those the which take up the
more in length and breadth than is wanting to them in height, ascending slopingly by degrees', while mountains are 'those the which with
an excessive height rise up towards the Skies'. Hills then are charac-
terized by rounded slopes, smooth in texture and soft in outline, and
mountains by abrupt changes of slope, rough in texture and harsh in
outline, and by crag and precipice; these distinctions are not always
borne out, however, by practical nomenclature. There should be a
difference in height, too. Mountains should be higher than hills, for
we often call the lower heights on the skirts of a mountain range, the
foothills. However, there is considerable variation and overlap, thus
Cairn Hill in Northumberland reaches 2,545 feet, while above the

plains of Anglesey a mere 450-foot eminence glories in the name, Parys Mountain.

In England and Wales the magic height, separating (perhaps) hills from mountains, has often been taken as 2,000 feet. Lists of mountains defined as all points above this height having at least one separate, and personal, contour line on the One Inch Ordnance Survey Map, have been published in climbing journals and there even exist doughty individuals who have ascended them all in painstaking years of effort. The grand total for England and Wales is 612 summits.

In Scotland the magic height selected by Sir Hugh Munro for his famous 'Tables' was 3,000 feet. He distinguished between separate mountains, numbering 283, and different summits on the same mountain, which added a further 255, a total of 538. These figures, incidentally, emphasize the relatively mountainous nature of Scotland, the corresponding figures for 3,000-foot mountains in England, Wales and Ireland being 7, 16 and 11 respectively. Munro's diligence has been rewarded by the now well-established use of his name for any Scottish mountain above 3,000 feet. Some stalwarts have climbed every peak on his list, but Munro himself fell short by two.

The native languages of the various mountain districts have produced a wide variety of names for hills and mountains, a selection of which is given below:

England: Beacon, Carn, Crag, Dodd, Down, Fell, Forest, Hill, Mount, Pen, Pike, Tor, Wold.

Wales: Allt, Aran, Blaen, Bryn, Carnedd, Carreg, Clogwyn, Craig, Crib, Drum, Esgair, Moel, Mynydd, Pen, Rhos.

Scotland: Beinn (Ben), Bidean, Binnean or Binnein, Braigh, Carn, Creag, Druim, Forest, Mam, Meall, Monadh, Sgurr(Sgor), Sron or Strone, Stac, Stuc, Stob.

Ireland: Beinn(Ben), Cnoc(Knock), Slieve.

The kinship between Crag, Craig, and Creag, Moel and Meall, etc. will be obvious. For other hill features the equivalents in the different tongues of 'pass' are bwlch, beallach and ballagh, while 'coombe' is rendered as cwm, corrie and coom. Pairs of hills are often distinguished as Great and Little in England, Fawr and Fach in Wales and Mor and Beag (or Beg) in Scotland and Ireland. Indeed most names are simply descriptive, such as Red Pike, Carnedd Goch and Carn Dearg, all of which in the various tongues mean 'red mountain'. Flights of fancy, like Pen Llithrig y Wrach, 'the slippery hill of the witch', are much less common. Sometimes names are doubled, as in Beacon Hill, or even trebled, Pendle Hill for example means 'Pen- hill- Hill'.

In early times hills often had different names on different sides. Certainly when the first Ordnance Surveyors came to question local inhabitants about names for the maps misunderstandings sometimes arose. For example, Cawsand Beacon on Dartmoor was originally Cosdon; in local accent this would sound like 'Kaaz'n' for which the surveyor wrote 'Cawsand', the name already given to a bay outside Plymouth Sound, 25 miles away.

In these densely populated islands where so many incompatible interests compete for the use of our mountain lands, preservation movements are of special importance and interest. As long as there was only limited pressure for the spoliation of scenery, preservation rested largely, whatever their motives, on the good sense of individual land-owners. Most of the problems which beset us today have arisen since the turn of the century. Currently there are four major movements concerned with preservation.

The National Trust, a private organization founded in 1895, is financed by endowment, legacies, donations and subscriptions. It owns 470 square miles of England and Wales including Rough Tor and St Agnes Beacon, Cissbury and Ditchling, Box and Leith Hills, the Clent Hills, Helsby Hill, Skirrid Fawr, Sugarloaf and the Clwydian Hills. The National Trust for Scotland, a separate body, also owns some mountain land.

The Forestry Commission, started in 1919, has established 2,000 square miles of woodland and owns altogether 4,000 square miles. A big planting programme lies ahead, mostly in hill and mountain areas. There are 460 forests throughout Britain including the National Forest Parks of Argyll, Dean, Snowdonia, Glen Trool, Glen More, Queen Elizabeth (Trossachs) and Border.

The very important National Parks and Access to the Countryside Act (1949) conferred on the Nature Conservancy extensive powers to create Nature Reserves. Around 190 square miles are thus controlled, including Cwm Idwal, Cader Idris, Tregaron Bog and some large areas in Scotland.

Under the same Act certain areas were set aside as National Parks, defined as:

> ... those extensive tracts of country in England and Wales as to which it appears that by reason of (a) their natural beauty and (b) the opportunities they afford for open-air recreation, having regard both to their character and to their position in relation to centres of population—it is especially desirable that the necessary measures should be taken for the purpose of preserving and enhancing their natural beauty and for the purpose of promoting their enjoyment by the public.

Ten National Parks, amounting to 5,254 square miles and including a high proportion of hill and mountain country, were designated during the subsequent years. A further 1,852 square miles were given a measure of protection as 'Areas of Outstanding Natural Beauty', while 1,028 miles of rights-of-way were promised over certain long-distance routes, such as the Pennine Way, Offa's Dyke, etc.

Unfortunately this splendid scheme largely foundered during its first decade. These amenity areas were precisely those coveted for water supply, hydroelectric generation, afforestation and service training, while in due course a nuclear power station, a ballistic missile early warning station, an oil refinery and numerous radio masts were also sited within Park boundaries. In the words of Lord Strang, Chairman of the National Parks Commission—'Where a government department has had plans for erecting large installations of one kind or another in a National Park, I can remember no case where it has been diverted from its purpose by anything the Commission might say about the intentions of Parliament as embodied in the National Parks Act.'

There is often a direct conflict also between the twin aims of enhancing natural beauty and of promoting the enjoyment of that beauty by the public. The latter with its cars, camp sites, accommodation and refreshment facilities and inevitable need for organization tends all the time to destroy exactly that which it was hoped to preserve. The car in particular has become a menace in the Park areas and is a threat to the whole system. There are many other problems—the exact standards to which we wish to preserve, the status and future of the people who live and work in the Parks, and so on. Some of the solutions are far

2 *Suilven from Lochinver*

from obvious and the discussions are too complicated to be detailed here.*

The wildlife of British mountains provides a complex study of its own, for which specialized texts are available.† Among the birds and animals the only truly montane species are the mountain hare, dotterel, ptarmigan and snow bunting. The last two only breed in the Northern Highlands; the mountain hare, once similarly confined, has now been reintroduced elsewhere. To these may be added the creatures of the high crags and screes—pine marten, fox, golden eagle, peregrine falcon, raven, buzzard and kite. The golden eagle, found in England 150 years ago, now only survives in the far north of Scotland. Only the fox, raven and peregrine falcon are found in all our mountain areas. The list of hill animals and birds is, of course, much longer and includes many which have been driven uphill from the plains. Extensive grazing by sheep has changed the whole pattern of vegetation in many upland areas, all but a fraction of which are covered now by bog, moorland and grassland. A wider variety of plants is found on exposed summit ridges, on screes and cliffs, in gullies and beside streams and springs. There are but few endemic species, most being derived either from Arctic sources or from the mountain ranges of Europe.

Only occasionally in the British Isles is the land flat as far as the eye can see. Mostly the landscape is diversified by hill and valley and broken up into limited vistas by hill crests which beckon us to discover what lies beyond. Even the lowest hills do this for us, and thus can become as important in our lives as higher hills which are farther away. Frank Smythe, the famous mountaineer, who knew well both the Alps and the Himalayas, once said of the Surrey Downs—'Those who love hills need go no higher than Holmbury's summit. They will discover there that height counts for little and that it is the hill that matters. The low hills teach us that height . . . is something precious'. All of us can win it in our various ways everywhere.

We begin our study of British hills in the west of Cornwall and, wandering back and forth over the land but moving ever northwards, end it 800 miles away in far-off Shetland.

*But see especially E. W. Hodge, *Enjoying the Lakes.*
†e.g. Various volumes in the Collins' *New Naturalist Series.*

ONE

England—West, South and East

The higher hills of Cornwall are found where four granite masses have been intruded among the slates and grits forming the bulk of the peninsula. These are the West Penwith area, forming the extreme tip of the county behind Land's End, the Carn Menellis Moors, south of Redruth, the St. Austell Moors and Bodmin Moor. All four have much in common—large tracts of moorland with an average height of 800 feet, mostly heather and peat bogs, strewn with weathered granite boulders and often surmounted by granite blocks 20 or 30 feet high, known as tors.

Mineral veins round the edges of the granite gave rise to the tin and copper mining industries for which the county was for long world-famous. Cornish tin was important even in prehistoric Britain bringing, among others, the Phoenicians to these shores. The Romans came here in their turn; one of their ingots is preserved in Truro Museum. In the early days the metal was obtained from ores at or near the surface, then during the eighteenth century the engines of Newcomen and Watt made possible the sinking and draining of the deep shafts and passages which honeycomb the land to this day. This phase was brief; more accessible foreign sources of tin stole the trade and by 1930 only a handful of mines remained. Now there are but two, and of the rest—huge areas of abandoned mine-scarred land, covered with gorse and bracken and riddled with overgrown shafts and tunnels, tottering ruins of engine houses and stamping mills and the characteristic mine chimney stacks.

The 'first and last' hill in England is Chapel Carn Brea (657 feet). Below is Land's End, the last angle of the land where the English

Channel meets the Bristol Channel, with ahead nothing but the Scillies and America. There are always small tramp steamers in view, paralleling the shore and passing inside or outside the Longships Lighthouse, from one side of England to the other. This is indeed a well signposted corner of the sea; Pendeen Light is only five miles to the north beyond Cape Cornwall, Wolf Rock a dozen miles to the south, while beyond the Scillies Bishop Rock, Peninnis Head and Round Island mark the farthest outposts of the land.

A range of hills runs parallel to the north coastline for ten miles or so to St Ives. Sandwiched between the north coast road and the hurrying miles of A30, this is a quiet land and one can enjoy in comfortable solitude the antiquities of Chûn Castle, the holed rock of Mên an Tol, the cromlech at Lanyon Quoit and the stone circles and hut villages. To the south St Michael's Mount with its castle dominates Mounts Bay, northwards are the great granite sea cliffs of the rock climbers. Around St Just was a great mining area; the ruins and the chimneys extend from the cliff edge up and over the hills, lonely and deserted now like the one at Ding Dong. Watchcroft (827 feet) is the highest point hereabouts.

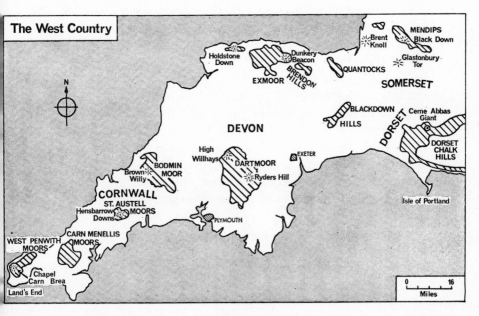

The greatest concentration of mines lies around Redruth above which the scarred slopes of Carn Brea are topped by a monument to Lord de Dunstanville. From here the moors extend southwards beyond Carn Menellis (819 feet). This area is important also for the quarrying of granite which has been used all over the country in the construction of harbours, bridges and lighthouses. Northward on the coast is the isolated St Agnes Beacon (619 feet) and Cornish legend has it that the giant Bolster used to stand with one foot here and one on Carn Brea. This is another mining area, but with wonderful views up and down the coast.

China clay, first discovered in Cornwall in 1755, is mined on the St Austell Moors (Hensbarrow Downs, 1,027 feet) and is exported in large quantities from the southern ports. The open conical pits are 300 feet deep or more. Waste products from the processing are piled alongside in huge white mounds, hundreds of feet high, on which vegetation only reluctantly grows. These, showing up from a great distance as in a view of the Alps from the plains of Europe, are often called 'the Cornish Alps'.

A30, with its summer flood of holiday cars, crosses the centre of Bodmin Moor, three miles from Brown Willy (1,375 feet) the highest point. Again the walker who leaves the road—and he certainly will not want to stay on it—will only have himself for company, and there are prehistoric remains and spacious views to the northern and southern seas. Farther south is Dozmary Pool, where Sir Bedivere was at length persuaded to dispose of the sword of King Arthur. The highest hill on this side of the Moor is Kilmar Tor (1,296 feet). Stowes Hill nearby is surmounted by a fantastic rock tor, the Cheesewring, while Caradon Hill a mile or so away has a TV mast. From these eastern summits the view extends across the Tamar to Devonshire and Dartmoor.

The largest and highest of the granite masses of the West Country falls within the Dartmoor National Park. This has an area of over 365 square miles, much of it bleak and treeless moorland. The trunk roads and railways to the west pass by on either side, but the main road from Tavistock to Ashburton bisects the Moor, running for several miles at over 1,000 feet with a summit of 1,431 feet near Princetown. In the northern portion are the highest hills—High Willhays (2,039 feet) and Yes Tor, half a mile away, 11 feet lower but a much more impressive mountain. The eight miles of high level moorland between here and Two Bridges include Hangingstone Hill (1,984 feet) and Cut Hill (1,981 feet), as well as many other points over 1,500 feet. South of the road the country is similar though not so high, reaching 1,692 feet at Ryders Hill, south of Dartmeet. As in Cornwall deposits of metalliferous ores and of china clay round the edges of the granite gave rise to comparable mining industries, but while there is still evidence of these in many places, the impression of devastation is not so widespread.

It has been contended that Dartmoor makes the greatest impression from a distance, when the hills seem to pile up one above the other into a massive mountain block; closer at hand the slopes are long and gentle and really striking features are lacking. This may well be so; yet mountains are much more than a backcloth to the view from the plains and they can only be completely appreciated by crossing their passes and their summits.

The tors surmounting the hills are higher and wider than those of Cornwall. In places, such as Great Staple Tor (1,482 feet) and Great Links Tor (1,908 feet) the rock mass forms the actual summit of the hill, which is thus accessible only to the rock climber. Below many of the tors is a slope of loose granite boulders called a clitter, broken off from the main crag by frost action at a time when conditions were much colder than they are today. Altogether there are about 170 tors, including Vixen Tor, near Merrivale, one of the few not actually on or near a ridge or summit, the tourist-stricken Haytor with staircase and handrail, Bowerman's Nose of grotesque shape, near Manaton, and Great Mis Tor, where there is a rock basin three feet in diameter and six inches deep referred to as long ago as 1291. Some of the rock forms are quite fantastic—one climber, for example, has reported 'a peak, presumably virgin, which is entirely round, an isolated rock some 12 or 15 feet high shaped like a football and absolutely without holds'.

Rock suitable for the climber is thinly spread. The weathering of many of the tors has left a series of bulging rounded layers, 'in the manner of the right hand profile of the letter B', and places which look climbable turn out to be holdless. The finest crag is the Dewerstone on the south-west side of the Moor, half a mile from Shaugh Bridge and only seven miles from Plymouth. It rises for 200 feet or more from a steeply sloping hillside directly above the River Plym. The valley is thickly wooded, but the crag far out-tops the trees; even if you do not climb it is a fine picnic spot. Haytor has climbs, so have Sheeps' Tor above Burrator Reservoir, Hound Tor, near Manaton, and the long side of Vixen Tor. But no one would come here just for the rock climbing.

Heavy rainfall and impervious rock near a surface covered with spongy peat lead to the formation of considerable areas of bog and marsh, many of which consist of islands, or hags, of peat and bog grass fissured by channels of bare, soggy earth. Such terrain is difficult to negotiate after considerable rainfall and involves continuous search for rifts narrow enough to jump. In certain places, and much more formidable, are so-called mires, where the ground is soft and quaking, or even semi-liquid underfoot and often covered with a layer of moss. In the northern part of the Moor a huge bog area is centred on Cut Hill and here rise the Devon rivers—Taw, Okement, Teign, Dart and Tavy, while a similar bog in the south is the source of the Avon, Plym and Erme. Here at the head of Swincombe is Fox Tor Mire, one of the few really dangerous bogs of Dartmoor—'Grimpen Mire' of the *Hound of the Baskervilles*.

In spite of all this wetness Dartmoor is remarkable for the absence of natural lakes. During the Ice Age the main sheet did not reach this far south and in consequence there is no evidence of the scouring action which has produced lake basins elsewhere in the country. There are man-made reservoirs at Burrator, Holne and Fernworthy.

Remains of early man are found all over the Moor, dating from a time when conditions in these uplands were drier and warmer than now and dense forests made the plains below uninhabitable. Particularly noteworthy are the pounds—walled enclosures with rows of stone huts and room as well for cattle and sheep—the best known of which is Grimspound, north of Widecombe. In addition there are stone avenues and circles, burial places of various kinds, camps and clapper bridges, the last a characteristic Dartmoor feature, bridging a stream with huge flat slabs of granite. The rock basins, to which we have already referred, were formerly attributed to the Druids, but in fact, they are a result of natural processes of weathering. The largest on the Moor is at Yes Tor near Gidleigh.

With all these things to see it can be appreciated that Dartmoor is fine walking country, more exciting and rewarding than its rather featureless slopes may first suggest. Haskett Smith described it as 'curious rather than beautiful, and more interesting to the geologist, the antiquary and the fisherman than to the mountaineer'. He added: 'It is instructive even to him, for the frequency of rain and mist and the paucity of landmarks which can be seen more than a few yards off, coupled with the necessity of constantly watching the ground, render it one of the easiest places in the world in which to lose one's way in any but the finest weather.' A crossing of the main part of the Moor from Okehampton or Belstone in the north to Ivybridge or South Brent is a particularly fine expedition. The distance is around 35 miles and should be comfortably possible in 12 hours or so in good conditions. The first objective is Cranmere Pool, six miles south of Okehampton. Before the Army built roads on the north side of the Moor to serve the Artillery Range Cranmere was a mysterious and somewhat inaccessible spot. Even to reach it was considered a worthy feat and a pillar box was set up there with a special rubber stamp so that the traveller could authenticate his visit. Now it is a mere mile from the road at Observation Point 15 on Okement Hill, from which it is hardly uphill at all, though still well camouflaged by the featureless moorland. The route goes on by the mires of Cut Hill and down the ridge west of the West Dart to Two Bridges. Down below alongside the river is Wistman's Wood, a famous four acres of stunted oak trees, 10 to 12 feet high and hundreds of years old, sprouting between the boulders of a clitter.

The main road, which is crossed here, could be used to divide the walk. Away to the south-west is Princetown with its ugly prison, erected in Napoleonic times to house prisoners of war, and its 750-foot television mast, symbol of modern enslavement to the television set, erected more recently. Leaving all this firmly behind, the route continues across South Hessary Tor and by Nun's Cross to Erme Head. In the upper Erme Valley is a stone row over two miles long, the longest on the Moor, while off to the left is Red Lake Mire with disused china clay workings. Ugborough Moor, between the Erme and the Avon, is then followed down to either Ivybridge or South Brent.

Away to the north the National Park of Exmoor has an area of 260 square miles. The hills, which are of Devonian slates and sandstones, are smooth and rounded and little rock is exposed at the surface. There are considerable areas over 1,400 feet; fields reach to 1,000 feet, above which is boggy moorland with grass, bracken and heather. Dunkery Beacon (1,707 feet), the highest point, carries a large cairn and the remains of the former beacon hearths; unfortunately a road runs within three-quarters of a mile and it is often visited by coach parties on summer days. They are rewarded by a view embracing Brown Willy, the Malvern Hills and the Black Mountains and Brecon Beacons in South Wales. There are many other places elsewhere on the Moor where the seclusion is shared only with wild ponies and red deer, except when the latter are being bloodthirstily hunted to death in an uneven contest curiously termed a sport.

The hill block ends abruptly close to the sea so that between Porlock and Ilfracombe there are only two villages reaching down to sea level—Lynmouth, clustered round the confluence of the East and West Lyns, and Combe Martin with its one-and-a-half-mile street winding up the valley of the Umber. Between Lynmouth and Combe Martin is some of the finest hog's back cliff scenery in the country, particularly where hills of over 1,000 feet—Great Hangman, Holdstone Down and Trentishoe Down—are only half a mile from the sea's edge. The seaward slopes of the hills are spread with a well-nigh impenetrable mantle of vegetation and access to the base is very difficult indeed. Experienced cliff climbers have worked out a traverse on the shore all along here, but it is specialized work suitable only for experts.

In 1869 R. D. Blackmore wrote the great Exmoor novel—*Lorna Doone*—full of magnificently rendered local colour and telling the story of a dangerous gang of ruffians said to have lived hereabouts in the seventeenth century. It seems unlikely that it had any factual basis but the background is certainly authentic. Blackmore's sites and scenes are typical rather than precise; the Badgeworthy Valley, south of County Gate, is nowadays called the Doone Valley though one or other of its tributaries more nearly fits the descriptions; Cloven Rocks Valley, where John Ridd finally overcame Carver Doone, is near Simonsbath.

Extending eastwards from Exmoor are the Brendon Hills (Lype Hill 1,391 feet)—similar country but at a somewhat lower level and more cultivated. These are separated from the ridge of the Quantock

Hills by a narrow strip of the Somerset Plain running from the Vale of Taunton Deane up to the coast at Watchet.

The Quantocks, rising to 1,262 feet at Will's Neck, run for 12 miles from north-west to south-east. Except for scrubby thorns, the tops are mostly treeless and covered with masses of heather; there are wooded coombes on the north-eastern slopes. Geologically this is an outlier of Exmoor–Devonian slates once again, and here also wild ponies and red deer flourish. This country was a rendezvous for poets and philosophers at the beginning of the last century, among them Coleridge who received hereabouts the inspiration for *The Ancient Mariner*.

To the south beyond the Vale of Taunton Deane rise the Blackdown Hills of East Devon with a monument to Wellington erected in 1817. To the north-west the Plain of Somerset extends across the field of Sedgemoor, where in 1685 the Duke of Monmouth lost the last battle fought in England, to the Polden Hills and beyond them to Cheddar and the Mendips. Two islands in the plain, Brent Knoll near Burnham and Glastonbury Tor (Avalon of the Arthurian legends), are surmounted by churches dedicated, like so many others on hill-tops, to St Michael.

Across the breadth of Somerset from Frome to the sea run the Mendip Hills, mainly Mountain Limestone with here and there a capping of Old Red Sandstone. Black Down (1,068 feet), south of Burrington Coombe, is the highest point. To the south lies the plain of the Axe, only a few feet above sea level, from which these hills rise wall-like in a landscape of grey rocks and grey stone walls, short turf and stunted hawthorn bushes, dry gorges and swallow holes.

There is no surface drainage on the limestone. The rainfall percolates into the rock and descends through fissures great and small to reappear at the hill foot. Cave explorers, entering high up on the tops at tiny openings like Swildon's Hole and Eastwater Swallet near Priddy, have penetrated by narrow squeezes and crawls, by a stream bed and water-fall, down ropes and ladders to points over 400 feet below the surface. Great streams flow out below, for example at Wookey Hole, where frogmen have followed the water into the hill for some hundreds of feet, but the exact interconnections are still a matter for speculation and it seems improbable that the way through can ever be forced by man. The glories of the world of caves can be sampled by everyone at Cheddar and at Wookey.

Early man used many of the smaller, drier caves as dwelling places and these have been painstakingly excavated to the great enrichment of the local museums. Along the watersheds from far-off Avebury came trackways along Mendip top to the sea, marked by a line of camps from Maesbury above Shepton Mallet to Worlebury near Weston. Metallic ores were an early discovery and when the Romans moved westwards they took over an already active lead mining industry. In the British Museum is a 'pig' of the metal which has been dated to A.D. 49. Mining continued for centuries and overgrown evidence of old workings is abundant all over the hills.

At Cheddar, where cheese has now partly given place to straw-berries, is the most spectacular of the gorges. The rock scenery on the near-vertical south wall, which rises over 400 feet above the road, is as fine as any in Britain. The gorges at Ebbor and at Burrington, where the Rev. Toplady found the cleft in the 'Rock of Ages' in 1762, are lesser, but correspondingly less people know of them. A little rock climbing has been done at Cheddar, but the rock is poor and danger-ously poised above the spectators who would quickly collect below. The most popular climbing crags in this part of the country rise delight-fully above the river and the municipal tennis courts in the Avon Gorge in the City of Bristol.

The annual rainfall in the Mendips is in no way excessive, yet on two separate occasions record amounts of more than nine inches of rain have fallen in a day hereabouts.

Broadly speaking, the hills of south-east England from the mouth of the Exe to the mouth of the Tees comprise two great geological groups. The Cretaceous rocks, of which chalk is the principal, lie mainly to the south-east of the Jurassic rocks, among which Oolitic Limestone pre-dominates. The limestone belt begins in Dorset where it forms the cliffs from Durlston Head almost to Bridport. There is chalk in some places, however, such as Worbarrow Bay and the chalk outcrops again beyond the limestone at Beer. The limestone sea cliffs at St. Alban's Head have provided some hard rock climbing, while the same rock rises to over 500 feet on the Isle of Portland, Hardy's 'Gibraltar of Wessex'. The outcrop of Jurassic rocks narrows between Frome and

4 Dartmoor—Yes Tor fro
Belstone Tor

Bruton to a pass between hills of chalk and Mountain Limestone, beyond which it broadens and rises to form the Cotswold Hills.

The Cotswolds run in an unbroken ridge for over 50 miles from Stinchcombe Hill above Dursley to Dover's Hill near Chipping Campden. The skyline is unbroken by gaps; the scarp faces towards the Valley of the Severn, the dip drops gently mile after mile until it sinks below the clays of the Vale of Oxford. The scarp face has receded leaving outliers of locally resistant rock in the form of hills on the plain such as Robin's Wood Hill and Churchdown. Haresfield Beacon and Stinchcombe Hill are at a less advanced stage and are still attached to the main range by a narrow isthmus. There are fine views everywhere over the plains to the Forest of Dean, May Hill and the Malverns. The highest point is Cleeve Common (1,083 feet), which has a golf course running up to and over the summit.

The vegetation is similar to that of the chalk downs with short turf and beech woods. Drayton called the range 'that great King of Shepherds', for in his day this was one of the great wool growing areas of England. He gives in *Polyolbion* a description of the countryside which is still significant today:

> *A Hill there holds his head, as though it told a tale,*
> *Or stooped to look down, or whisper with a Vale;*
> *Where little purling winds like wantons seem to dally,*
> *And skip from bank to bank, from valley trip to valley.*
> *Such sundry shapes of Soil where Nature doth devise,*
> *That she may rather seem fantastical than wise.*

The bare rock is exposed in a few places and a little climbing has been done. There is a notable pinnacle, called the Devil's Chimney, above Leckhampton, from which unwary tourists are periodically rescued, after finding that a descent with its downward views is considerably more daunting than the buoyantly approached ascent. This Oolitic Limestone is a particularly happy building stone and Cotswold villages are widely famed for their harmony and colour. Massingham has written—'Raw beneath the soil, it is of a most delicate buff colour, deepening in certain conditions to orange, but, after weathering and long exposure, it tones to a warm soft silvery grey . . . The transformation of the stone from buff to grey affects its surface, so that,

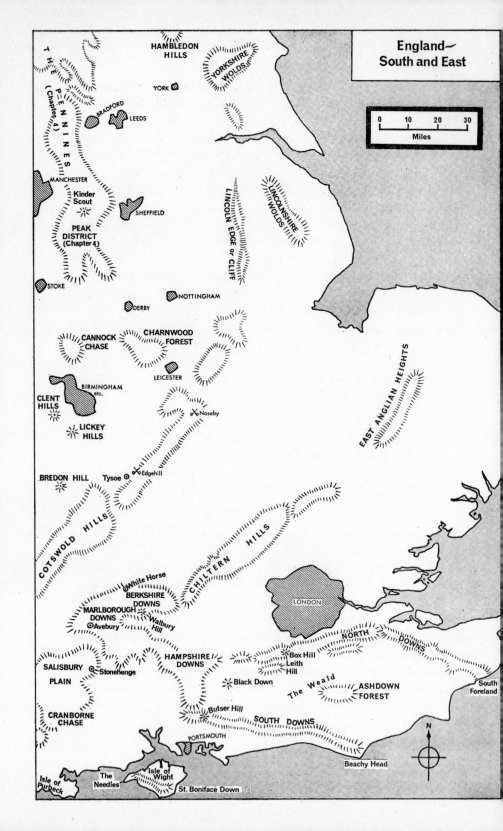

England — South and East

THE PENNINES (Chapter 4)

HAMBLEDON HILLS

YORKSHIRE WOLDS

YORK

BRADFORD
LEEDS

0 10 20 30
Miles

MANCHESTER

Kinder Scout

SHEFFIELD

PEAK DISTRICT (Chapter 4)

LINCOLN EDGE or CLIFF

LINCOLNSHIRE WOLDS

STOKE

NOTTINGHAM

DERBY

CANNOCK CHASE

CHARNWOOD FOREST

CLENT HILLS

BIRMINGHAM etc.

LICKEY HILLS

LEICESTER

Naseby

EAST ANGLIAN HEIGHTS

BREDON HILL
Tysoe
Edgehill

COTSWOLD HILLS

CHILTERN HILLS

LONDON

White Horse

BERKSHIRE DOWNS

MARLBOROUGH DOWNS

Avebury

Walbury Hill

NORTH DOWNS

SALISBURY PLAIN

Stonehenge

HAMPSHIRE DOWNS

Box Hill
Leith Hill

Black Down

The Weald

ASHDOWN FOREST

South Foreland

CRANBORNE CHASE

Butser Hill

SOUTH DOWNS

PORTSMOUTH

Beachy Head

N

Isle of Purbeck

The Needles

Isle of Wight

St. Boniface Down

sole among limestones, it possesses the quality of retaining the light
and so of quickening and responding to the moods of light.'

Dover's Hill at the northern end was the site of a festival of old
English sports 'The Olympick Cotswold Games' founded in the
reign of James I by Robert Dover, a local man of law, and continuing
up to 1851.

Bredon Hill (960 feet), an outlier of the main range, rises in isolation
between Evesham and Tewkesbury. This is one of those special hills
which by virtue of grand form or isolated position seem to dominate
their surroundings and thus influence the thinking and writing of people
who look on them far beyond the proportion of their mere size and
height. In some famous and poignant lines the local poet A. E. Housman wrote:

> *And see the coloured counties*
> *And hear the larks so high*
> *About us in the sky,*—the scenic background to a tragedy.

Many years before Drayton had noted Bredon as a good example of
the stature that hills derive from the proximity of flat plains, amor-
ously embraced, as he put it, in the arms of the Vale of Evesham:

> *And when great Malvern looks most terrible and grim,*
> *Bredon with a pleased brow continually doth smile.*

Before continuing along the line of the Jurassic outcrop towards the
north we turn aside momentarily to look at one or two isolated hill
groups in the Midland plain which are of particular interest. A few
miles north of Leicester are the 'aged antique rocks' of Charnwood
Forest—granites, slates and volcanic ashes, which rise to 1,000 feet
or so above the clays of the plain. These are the remains of very ancient
mountains, once buried, now exposed again. Bare rock shows through
in places and the slopes covered with woods and bracken contrast
markedly with the fertility of the plain. North of the Forest is Bredon-
on-the-Hill—a real etymological mix-up as both parts of 'Bredon' mean
'hill'. The church here is on the crest of a steep hill above the village;
it was intended to build it in the village but every night 'doves' (*sic*)
carried the stones up to the hill-top. Nearby there used to be some good
climbing on dolomite limestone in a quarry.

The Lickey Hills (965 feet) close to Birmingham are of similar antiquity. Drayton noted them as 'supposed to be the highest ground of this Isle not being a Mountain', but he may well have been confusing them with the nearby Clent Hills which reach 1,036 feet south-west of Birmingham. In the Railway Age one of the steepest gradients on the standard system (1 in 37) took the Birmingham to Gloucester line over the Lickey Hills. For many years additional engines stood by here to push the trains over the bank, until finally in 1919 an 0–10–0 'Decapod' was specially designed for the job by Sir Henry Fowler. This was known as 'The Lickey Banker' and was until the advent of British Railways in 1948 the only engine in the country with five sets of coupled wheels.

The general trend of the Cotswold ridge is continued in a northerly direction by an outcrop of the limestone known as marlstone. This forms the escarpment at Edgehill, north-west from Banbury, where the first inconclusive battle of the Civil War was fought in 1642. The Royalist army charged down the slope of the hill to attack the Parliamentary troops in the valley. Nearby was the Red Horse of Tysoe, the only hill figure cut in any rock other than chalk, which disappeared around 1800, leaving as the only reminder the name—Vale of the Red Horse—for the valley below. The scarp line continues through Northamptonshire seldom rising above 700 feet, passes the battlefield of Naseby where the results were only too conclusive, and so into Leicestershire. Beyond Grantham begins the strange ridge known as Lincoln Edge, or Cliff, which continues the outcrop of limestone-type rocks towards the north. This seldom exceeds 150 feet in height and is hardly a hill at all, yet it leads us straight on to the final outcrop of the Jurassic system—the North Yorkshire Moors.

This compact mountain block forms a National Park with an area of some 600 square miles, between the Vale of York to the west, the Vale of Pickering to the south and the quadrant of coastline between Scarborough and Middlesbrough. Most of this is heather-covered moorland over 1,000 feet high with its highest point (1,450 + feet) close to the head of Bransdale. This is a north-country Dartmoor, but lacking completely the large numbers of tourists of the west country. North and south sides are cut up by steep-sided narrow valleys; the ridges between are rounded and smooth in outline and the roads follow them in preference to the valleys. Such a road is that which climbs from Castleton in the north by the ridge of Castleton Rigg to a summit at 1,360 feet and descends by Blakey Rigg to Hutton-le-Hole and the Vale of Pickering. At the summit the antique Ralph Cross has a hollow on top in which alms were once placed for travellers; nowadays passers-by leave pennies there for children.

The Jurassic rocks include others besides limestone. In fact extensive ironstone deposits were worked here years ago and account for the rise of the industrial area of Middlesbrough. The coast from Filey to Saltburn shows some fine cliffs, that at Boulby claiming to be the highest sea cliff in England. The north-western part of the Moors is known as the Cleveland Hills (derived from 'Cliffland') and here there are several rock exposures, mostly sandstones, which are used by climbers. The best known is the Wainstones on Hasty Bank. A few miles farther north shapely Roseberry Topping, the 'Matterhorn of Cleveland', towers to a height of, unfortunately, only 1,057 feet. Easby Moor a mile or so away carries a memorial column to Captain Cook, born nearby. At the western edge of the Park the Hambledon Hills look down on the Vale of York. There is a fine view across this to the Pennines from Sutton Bank on the Thirsk road, while gliders soar overhead in the up-currents created by the scarp. This steepens to vertical at Roulston Scar, which is, however, too rotten for the climber.

Most of the Park is splendid walking country. A noteworthy expedition is the so-called Lyke Wake Walk which runs from Osmotherly in the west to Ravenscar on the coast, a distance of some 40 miles, and crosses most of the highest points on the Moor. This takes its name from the dirge which used to be sung for the dead whose souls passed this way. In these modern times the new scientific monstrosity on Fylingdales Moor robs this fine walk of some of its original fascination. The countryside everywhere is filled with reminders of our precarious existence, either in the form of relics left behind from previous World Wars or advanced technological preparations for the next. Nowhere are these brought more obviously to our attention than here. Should missiles come these gigantic radar aerials will give us another minute or two to get used to the idea of the fate in store for us.

In south-east England the older rocks of the west dip far below the surface. On top lies a huge thickness of newer rocks of which chalk is by far the most widespread. It is in fact a pure limestone, white and relatively soft, consisting of fragments of sea-shells deposited originally on the bed of some ancient sea. Interspersed through the chalk are nodules of silica called flints. Where chalk forms the surface of the land we find characteristic scenery of close turf with juniper bushes, dry valleys and smooth whale-backed hills, contrasting sharply with the wooded or cultivated lowlands beneath. Elsewhere, where the topsoil is derived from other materials such as gravel or clay-with-flints, which is debris left when the chalk itself is dissolved away, the hills themselves are either wooded or cultivated and farms and villages are more widely distributed.

The centre of the chalk country is Salisbury Plain, a rolling treeless plateau of bare slopes and distant views, spoiled to some extent by military activities. This focal area extends northwards to include the Marlborough Downs beyond the Vale of Pewsey and eastwards to the Hampshire-Berkshire border. That this was the heart of prehistoric England is testified by the considerable remains of stone circles, camps, trackways and burial places (long and round barrows) on every hand. Early man found here ample opportunity for cultural progress, well-drained land adapted for cultivation, flints for the fabrication of implements and easily worked rock to build habitations and fortifications. The two most famous ritual centres are now in the capable hands of the Ministry of Public Buildings and Works. The Stone Circle at Avebury with its ditch and bank, 3,000–4,000 years old and the largest in Europe, lies half-way between Marlborough and Calne. To the south is Stonehenge near Amesbury, constructed over 4,000 years ago partly from local stone and partly from rocks brought from Prescelly Mountain in Pembrokeshire.

From this central area the chalk spreads out in a series of radiating ridges—the South Downs, which run across the breadth of south Sussex to the sea at Beachy Head; the North Downs, facing the South Downs across the whole length of the Weald and ending in the white cliffs of the North and South Forelands; a long line of hills comprising the Berkshire Downs and the Chiltern Hills, which continues at a lower level through East Anglia to Hunstanton and though broken by the

Wash and the Humber, culminates in the Yorkshire Wolds; and finally a broad line running south-westwards through Cranborne Chase into Dorset, which, turning east through the Isle of Purbeck, forms finally the backbone of the Isle of Wight. These were the causeways, drier and more open than the marshy overgrown plains below, followed by the prehistoric trackways which crossed the length and breadth of southern England.

Nowhere do the chalk hills reach 1,000 feet. Inkpen Beacon, south of the Kennet Valley in Berkshire, for long credited with 1,011 feet, was demoted during the last century to 955 feet and the highest chalk hill is in fact the nearby Walbury Hill (975 feet). Milk Hill on the Marlborough Downs reaches 964 feet and is the highest point in Wiltshire. From Inkpen to Milk Hill and on towards Somerset runs the Wansdyke, a defensive ditch and bank built to protect the south-west against invaders from the north. There is no record of what sort of struggles it has seen. A struggle there certainly was much later in history on Roundaway Down north-east of Devizes, where the Cavaliers defeated Waller and his Roundheads in 1643.

The South Downs show over their length of 60 miles exactly what we expect chalk hills to be. Gilbert White (1720–1793), the celebrated early naturalist, who lived closeby at Selborne, called them 'that chain of majestic mountains' and once Hampshire is left behind, this is indeed what they are. On a warm summer's day the hills seem to sleep peacefully enough in the sun, but when driving rain and moving curtains of mist alternately obscure and reveal their flanks they look every inch a mountain range. The northern scarp slope tumbles steeply into the Weald for miles on end, while southwards the sea is never very far away. It is magnificent country for the walker, who on the way can visit the camps at the Trundle, Cissbury and Chanctonbury Rings, Devil's Dyke and elsewhere as well as the huge 'Long Man' carved on the hillside at Wilmington. Chanctonbury carries a clump of beech trees (planted in 1860) which gives it a characteristic outline from near and far. The walker can see everything, but some excellent viewpoints are accessible also to the motorist from roads across the range and through the gaps. That there should be gaps through the chalk, apparently cut by the Wealden rivers in order to reach the sea is puzzling at first, until we realize that the cutting process started when the Weald area to the north was covered by a dome of still softer rocks and as this was worn away, the gaps in the chalk hills became deeper and deeper. The highest point, Butser Hill (889 feet), is at one end near the Petersfield—Portsmouth Road; at the other end the Downs are sharply sliced off by the sea to terminate in a series of vertical cliffs. Here Beachy Head is the only remaining unspoiled coastal scenery in south-east England, as well as being the only place where there is record of climbing on natural chalk.

The North Downs appear first at the Hog's Back between Guildford and Farnham. Thenceforward, apart from river gaps similar to those of the South Downs, the hill line is continuous between 600 and 800 feet almost to Canterbury. The ancient Harroway ran along here mostly at the foot of the scarp from Salisbury Plain to the Straits of Dover; later the pilgrims wending their way 'from every shires ende of Engelond to Caunterbury' used the same trackways for their journeys. The scarp is on the south side, while the dip slope runs down into the London Basin and is now considerably built over in the gradual spread of London's dormitories. Many Londoners come to these Downs at week-ends, or indeed most days, by foot, bicycle or car; Box Hill at Dorking, named for its box trees, is a much-visited viewpoint. In many places private land and houses bar access to the highest tops and it is not so easy to make such long continuous walks as can be done on the South Downs. These hills too terminate abruptly in the 'white cliffs' of eastern Kent.

Before we leave the Weald we still have to note the sandstone hills formed in the older, harder rocks exposed there by the removal of the chalk dome. The Lower Greensand forms hills near Hindhead, which rise to 918 feet at the tree-covered Black Down; farther east where the same rock outcrops parallel to the North Downs, again with a scarp on the south, Leith Hill is 965 feet and a summit tower provides the only point above 1,000 feet in the Home Counties. In the central Weald the Ashdown Sand reaches about 800 feet at Crowborough, and outcrops of this rock at lower levels provide the nearest rock climbing to London.

The Berkshire Downs have their scarp on the north side above the Vale of the White Horse. A notable feature is Uffington Hill (956 feet) with a camp on the summit and the most famous and the most

6 *The South Downs—near Lew*

antique of the white horses (1st century B.C.) carved on its flanks. During the last century the so-called 'scouring of the white horse', the clearing of weeds, etc., was carried out periodically and this was made the occasion for local sports and jollifications such as chasing a round cheese bowled down the hill, fighting with single-sticks and so on. Below the horse is one of the sites where St George may have slain the dragon, while a mile or so to the west is Wayland Smith's Cave, the remains of a cromlech. Following the Downs to the east we reach Goring Gap, where the river Thames breaks through the chalk ridge.

Beyond now are the Chiltern Hills, which continue in a 600- to 800-foot ridge as far as Dunstable. These are largely beech tree covered though slopes of bare chalk do protrude in places. Whiteleaf Cross, carved in the hillside above Princes Risborough, may be of considerable antiquity, but farther on there is a very modern carved lion which locates the zoo at Whipsnade. Dunstable Downs are used for gliding—presumably they take good care not to land within the zoo's perimeter. The Icknield Way, which has followed all these ridges from Wiltshire, continues along the lower hills far into East Anglia towards the flint mines at Brandon and the Wash. In Lincolnshire the Wolds reach 548 feet north of Market Rasen. Beyond the Humber there is another typical chalk area—the Yorkshire Wolds (South Wold 808 feet). There are scarp faces above the Vales of York and Pickering and the chalk finally ends at the high sea cliffs around Flamborough Head.

The last great arm of the chalk system starts south westwards from Salisbury Plain in the wooded uplands of Cranborne Chase (Win Green Hill, 911 feet). Camps at Hambledon Hill, Hod Hill and Badbury look down on the River Stour, beyond which the chalk continues to Bulberrow Hill (902 feet) and fine views over the Plain of Somerset. Farther west at Cerne Abbas is another carved giant, possibly a figure of Hercules dating from the second century A.D. 'Glorying in his strength and advertising his virility', carrying a huge club, he has been described as 'ithyphallic and clavigerous'. The chalk line sweeps round Dorchester and we arrive at the magnificent Maiden Castle, the most extensive and ingeniously contrived earthwork in the country. It is 900 yards long, 400 yards wide and has sometimes three, sometimes four tiers of ramparts and ditches with complex defences at the entrances. The chalk hills continue eastwards through the Isle of Purbeck, where Corfe Castle is built in a gap in the range. Old Harry Rocks, north of Swanage, mark the termination of the mainland, but the outcrop continues in the famous Needles in the Isle of Wight and in the central range of chalk hills there which culminates in St Boniface Down (787 feet).

TWO

The Border and Wales

The Welsh border counties of Gloucester, Hereford, Worcester and Shropshire show a varied collection of hill groups. These we shall now consider in turn, leaving until later some of those more obviously linked with the Welsh mountains, but borrowing on occasions hill groups from Wales which fall more appropriately here. Offa's Dyke, a linear fortification of the eighth century, 15 feet high in places, ran up through this country from the Wye to the Dee and traces can still be found, notably near Knighton. This 'mighty mound athwart from sea to sea' has been set aside as a long-distance footpath and, it is hoped, rights-of-way will eventually be established over its whole length.

The Forest of Dean in western Gloucestershire is wedged between the lower reaches of the Rivers Severn and Wye. This is Old Red Sandstone and Mountain Limestone with some gritstone and coal measures and is the second largest expanse of woodland in the Kingdom. 22,000 acres of it now form a National Forest Park; there is a small coalfield somewhere in the midst of the trees. The hills here reach 700 feet or so, but, between the Wye and the Usk, there is a point above 1,000 feet near Wentworth. The spectacular scenery hereabouts is provided by the limestone gorges of the Wye, notably at Symond's Yat and Wintour's Leap, where some climbing is done.

Hereford is an undulating county with many minor hills up to 1,000 feet and occasionally higher. Sometimes the summits are difficult of access, surrounded as they are by cultivation on all sides; it is a quiet and friendly county. Notice particularly the sharp turns in the River Lugg where it runs round the shoulder of Dinmore Hill near Hope-under-Dinmore, the double wall of hills which surrounds Woolhope, and farther south the wooded May Hill prominent in the view from the Cotswolds and the Severn Plain.

The beacon on the Malvern Hills was one of the many awaiting the Spanish Armada when it appeared off the West Country in 1588, and soon 'twelve fair counties saw the blaze on Malvern's lonely height'. The fires were undoubtedly sited on the Worcestershire Beacon, which at 1,395 feet is the highest point both of the ten-mile-long ridge and of the county. There is a summit indicator and the view embraces three cathedrals and the sites of six decisive British battles. As befits so outstanding a range the Malverns span centuries of history, for here, as related by William Langland in the fourteenth century, the vision came to Piers the Plowman:

Ac on a May morning on Malverne hilles
Me bifel a ferly . . .

and centuries later inspiration came likewise on these same slopes to the young Edward Elgar.

The rock is Pre-Cambrian gneiss and outcrops of this very ancient rock are quarried in places. Defoe thought that gold and silver might be here for the finding and that 'Mauvern would outdo Potosi for wealth', but, he added, ''tis probable that if there is such wealth, it lies too deep for this idle generation to find out, and perhaps to search for'. It still has not been found.

The word 'Malvern' is derived from the Welsh words *moel* (bald) and *bryn* (hill). From here to Wales is the breadth of a county, yet this is perhaps the beginning of the hills; on the one side is the plain of England, on the other hill after hill is backed by mountain after mountain. Northwards Woodbury Hill and Abberley Hill, both over 900 feet, are outliers of the range.

The striking Clee Hills rising to the north-east of Ludlow are pro-tected from erosion by caps of basalt, which have been quarried for road metal, so-called Dhu Stone. Titterstone Clee Hill (1,749 feet) with its camp and quarries commands a tremendous view southwards; Brown Clee Hill (1,790 feet) farther north is the highest point in Shropshire. The camp on this summit, known as Abdon Burf, has now been largely quarried away. Across Corve Dale are Aymestry Ridge and Wenlock Edge:

> *Wenlock Edge was umbered*
> *And bright was Abdon Burf*
> *And warm between them slumbered*
> *The smooth green miles of turf.*

Thus A. E. Housman, though it is said that when he penned these lines he had never been in Shropshire!

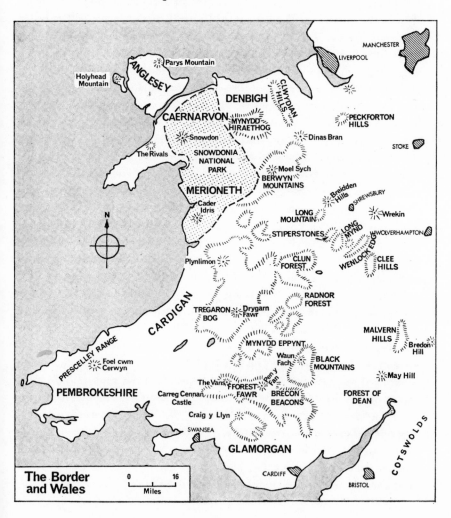

The Border and Wales

Wenlock Edge runs in a straight line for 17 miles from Much Wenlock in the north-east to Stokesay in the south-west. The average height is 750–800 feet with slightly higher summits in places. The rock is richly fossiliferous Silurian limestone and the north-westerly face above Ape Dale is steep, almost precipitous. A mile away there is a parallel ridge in the Aymestry Limestone, which reaches to over 1,000 feet. Hope Dale lies between the ridges and beyond the Aymestry Ridge are the wide undulating fields of Corve Dale.

Church Stretton stands in the centre of the hill country of Shropshire—one of the most pleasant and varied of the lesser hill areas of England. To the east rise Caer Caradoc (1,506 feet), Ragleth Hill, Hope Bowdler Hill and the Lawley, a range of Pre-Cambrian lavas, with small outcrops of shattered rock. West of the town is the ridge of the Long Mynd, a variety of Pre-Cambrian rocks reaching to 1,696 feet. The heather-clad slopes on this side are broken up by deep hollows, with rock-strewn streams and even waterfalls, of which the loveliest are Ashes Hollow and the Cardingmill Valley. On the other side the far slope looking to the Stiperstones and to Wales is straight, steep and smooth like the scarp on a chalk down. The top is a plateau, traversed from end to end by the ancient Portway, now a metalled road.

Prominent in the view from all these hills, away to the north-east lies the isolated Wrekin (1,335 feet). Many years ago, the Devil set out with a large spadeful of earth to dam the Severn and flood Shrewsbury. Reaching Wellington, and already tired and discouraged, he met a shoe-mender, carrying a bag full of worn-out shoes:

'How much farther to Shrewsbury?'

'Just look how many pairs of shoes I have worn out on the way' was the reply. The spadeful was thrown down without more ado forming the Wrekin, while the earth shaken from the boots of the Devil formed the Ercall nearby. The hill is made of very ancient rock, which is exposed in one or two places, and there are some rock climbs. This was an obvious site for a beacon and in 1588, soon after that on Malvern, there 'streamed in crimson on the wind the Wrekin's crest of light'. A modern beacon was erected here in World War II as a navigational aid for aircraft and left in position afterwards. The local people grew fond of its winking red light, and a proposal in 1964 to switch it off permanently aroused considerable opposition.

Parallel to the Long Mynd and farther west is another great ridge line, the Stiperstones. The rock here is quartzite, the summit 1,731 feet. A few 20- to 30-foot outcrops are perched on the backbone of the ridge. One of the most massive is called the Devil's Chair, and legend has it that the surrounding boulders dropped from his apron when he got up after resting there. Isolated hills rise close to both ends. Corndon Hill in the south is a dolerite laccolite, Pontesford Hill over towards Shrewsbury has a crag giving climbs up to 200 feet.

Long Mountain, over the Severn from Welshpool, is a smooth whaleback of Silurian sandstone which reaches 1,338 feet. This is presumably the same word as Long Mynd and it is odd therefore that the hills with the English name are in Wales, while those with the Welsh name are in England. Farther north beside the Severn are those shapely miniature mountains—the Breidden Hills, where Moel y Golfa reaches 1,324 feet. Hereabouts is believed to be the site of the last battleground of Caractacus, while centuries later the victories of Rodney in the 1780s were commemorated by a column on the top of the hill. The rock is Ordovician volcanic.

*　　*　　*　　*　　*

Northwards and westwards from the Forest of Dean the hills rise ever higher. Northern Monmouthshire is pastoral country with hills, such as Garway and Serrerthin, of 1,000 feet or so. As in the neighbouring Hereford some summits are hard to reach unless the climber is prepared to thread his way round cultivated fields. Craig Serrerthin looks particularly awkward of access, the middle parts trackless and clothed in high bracken, fern and stunted bushes.

Abergavenny, sited where the Gavenny joins the Usk, has hills on all sides. To the north-east Skirrid Fawr (1,601 feet) rises in isolation; two stones amid grass and whortleberries on the summit mark the site of yet another St Michael's Church. Northwards is the Sugarloaf (a popular name for mountains of simple conical shape); the south-west is blocked by the great bulk of the Blorenge. A road into the coal valley of Blaenavon almost crosses the summit of the latter, enabling everyone to enjoy a fine view of valley and mountain heightened by the sharp contrast between the north and south sides.

Beyond the Sugarloaf the Black Mountains rise in great rounded whale-backs. The scarp slope is on the north side above the Wye; the dip slope on the other is divided by a series of river valleys all draining to the south-east. In the best known of these, the Honddu, are the famous ruins of Llanthony Abbey and at Cwmyoy the only climbers' crag hereabouts; a narrow motor road crosses the hills at the valley head to Hay-on-Wye. In 1188, Giraldus wrote of Llanthony:

> . . . although it is on every side surrounded by lofty mountains, not stony or rocky, but of a soft nature, and covered with grass, Parian stones are frequently found there, and are so-called free stones from the facility with which they admit of being cut and polished, and with these the church is beautifully built. It is also wonderful, that when, after a diligent search, all the stones have been removed from the mountains, and no more can be found, upon another search, a few days afterwards, they reappear in greater quantities to those who seek them.

The highest point of this block, Waun Fach (2,660 feet), lies farther west above Talgarth.

The Blorenge is the first in a long range of mountains which stretches from here for some 40 miles on into Carmarthenshire. The pattern of the Black Mountains is repeated—steep slopes on the north, gentle slopes to the south dissected by parallel valleys. South of Brecon are the Brecon Beacons with Pen y Fan (2,907 feet) the highest point in South Wales. Roads on either side of the Beacons cross the range at over 1,400 feet, that to the east also carries a railway now unfortunately closed to passenger traffic. Here once the lucky railway passenger could ride behind the labouring engine puffing its way up the long 7-mile slope from 300 feet at pastoral Tal-y-Bont beside the Usk to more than 1,200 feet at Torpantau on the moorland slopes of the Beacons, then in a few miles of free-wheeling plunge down to the grim coal valleys of Merthyr Tydfil and Rhymney.

Pen y Fan, and the adjacent summits of Corn Du and Cribyn, throw down great crags on the north side—alternate layers of sandstone and shale where the edges of the Old Red Sandstone beds are exposed. These loose and uncertain faces are completely unsuitable for rock climbing, though they might be scaled by anyone foolhardy enough to ignore the obvious dangers. Occasionally in the depths of winter

8 *The Brecon Beac*

there is a different story to tell; ice binds together the fragments of rock and with the aid of an ice axe and some pitons an interesting alpine-type ascent can perhaps be enjoyed, as R. G. Sandeman, for example, has described. Even this is not without its terrors:

> . . . Standing on Davies's shoulders I got a grip at full arm's length upon the frozen turf along the top of the barrier. But I could only reach it with my finger-tips and Davies had to give me a push with his ice axe to enable me at last to draw myself up till I was lying gasping on the edge of the top. In this precarious position I found that there was no hold by which I could drag myself up to the almost vertical slope above. My half frozen fingers scraped and dug into the snow . . . and I somehow wriggled upwards with the point of my axe driven into the frozen turf above.

However, these things are seldom done as, rather than come from a distance on the chance of finding good conditions here, climbers prefer to go to the higher hills of North Wales.

Between the top of the Beacons and the sea the successive geological beds form a syncline, the Old Red Sandstone dipping far below the surface of the land. Above it is a thick layer of Mountain Limestone with many fine caves, then the coal measures for which this area is widely famous. Above these the Pennant Sandstone forms bleak moorland hills which rise to 1,969 feet at Craig-y-Llyn, the highest point in Glamorganshire, near the head of the Rhondda Valley. Mines and houses are confined to the valleys, which are often narrow and steep sided; the moors between remain in a comparatively wild state—a countryside this of wide contrasts. As one writer has remarked, it is less spoilt than the Black Country, for 'it is possible to walk in about ten minutes from any pithead into deep cwms, to wander over virgin hill-sides and beside crystal clear streams'.

Between the Craig-y-Llyn moors and the higher mountains of the Old Red Sandstone lies the beautiful Vale of Neath, with waterfalls which compare favourably with those in more touristy parts of Wales. The 'holes', which make this one of the major caving areas of Britain, are in the upper valleys of the Tawe, the Neath and the Mellte. Dan yr Ogof, open in part to the public, and Ogof Ffynnon Ddu with nearly 1½ miles of passages, both near Craig y Nos Castle, are among the best known. In Porth yr Ogof the River Mellte flows underground for

The Source of the River Wye   51
n Plynlimon

several hundreds of feet. Underground lakes, explored by coracle or rubber dinghy, seem to be the local forte; but there is other stern stuff also, for example the pothole at Pwll Dfwn in the Tawe Valley is 340 feet deep, while Agen Allwedd near Llangattock now has 14 miles of passages.

The scarp line of the Beacons, now called the Fforest Fawr, continues for many miles westwards past Fan Fawr and Fan Gehirych to terminate finally in the Brecknock and Carmarthen Vans, south of Llandovery. The former rises directly above Llyn y Fan Fawr, the source of the Tawe, in which there are said to be no fish. The latter rising similarly above Llyn y Fan Fach is the highest mountain in Carmarthenshire at 2,460 feet, though in fact not the highest ground as the border runs over a shoulder of the Brecknock Van to a height of some 2,550 feet. Close to Llandilo is the picture-book castle of Carreg Cennen perched on a rocky knoll, precipitous on all sides but one, and steep even there. The ruins are inconsiderable but the situation wonderful. There are wide views of mountain and valley and an interesting gallery cut in the rock leads down to the castle water supply.

The whole of the mountain area from Carreg Cennen to the eastern edge of the Black Mountains on the Herefordshire border is now the Brecon Beacons National Park—515 square miles of preservation, which may stay that way if we are lucky and no one in authority wants it for anything else.

Defoe was particularly impressed by these South Welsh mountains, writing of them:

> ... the Andes and the Alps, though immensely high, yet they stand together, and they are as mountains, piled upon mountains, and hills upon hills; whereas sometimes we see these mountains rising up at once, from the lowest valleys, to the highest summits, which makes the height look horrid and frightful, even worse than those mountains abroad, which though much higher, rise as it were, one behind another; so that the ascent seems gradual, and consequently less surprising.

In recent years all the points above 2,600 feet have been traversed in one continuous expedition on several occasions. It is about 35 miles. The cross-country runners do not seem to have tackled this one yet, so that the times, 12 hours or so, are still strictly those for walkers.

The continuous scarp edge makes this an interesting tramp, though it is spoiled to some extent in the latter stages by the unavoidable road walk between the Beacons and the Black Mountains. Thus the modern traveller skims lightly over the hills where Defoe found 'a ridge of horrid rocks and precipices, over which, if we had not had a trusty guide, we should never have found our way'.

We have to travel farther west beyond the River Towy, almost to Pembrokeshire, before we reach the next considerable hill group. The Prescelly Range crosses this county from east to west with its highest point, Foel Cwm Cerwyn (1,760 feet), easily accessible from the summit of the minor road from Eglwyswrw to Haverfordwest. The hills are rounded and give easy walking with distant views of the sea in three directions. It is said that in exceptional conditions one can see Dunkery Beacon, 76 miles south-east, Snowdon, 85 miles north-north-west, and the coast of Ireland. The large stones at Stonehenge came from this district, four of rhyolite from Carn Alw, the remainder of dolerite from Carn Meini. There are small natural exposures of rock at Treffgarne and elsewhere but few records of climbing. A series of low hills, monadnocks of very ancient rocks, rising out of a flat plain on the cliff-top near St David's are also worthy of mention—Pen Bery, Pen Llechwen, etc. The Prescelly Range and a coastal strip all round the county form the Pembrokeshire Coast National Park of 225 square miles. A continuous cliff-top path is planned, but the Castlemartin area, firmly in the hands of the military, is an obstacle unlikely to be shifted by mere considerations of amenity or of public feeling.

Between the Brecon Beacons and Cader Idris above Dolgellau is an extensive plateau area reaching up to and over 2,000 feet in places, of markedly uniform height and dissected in all directions by river valleys. From below there is perhaps no particular impression of uniformity but it becomes immediately obvious in the view from higher hill-tops such as Plynlimon. There are some distinctive groups, such as the Mynydd Eppynt, 1,550 + feet, north of Brecon, which is crossed by one road reaching 1,493 feet near the northern edge. The Drovers' Arms on this same road reminds us that cattle and sheep were once driven this way towards markets in England. Some of this area is now artillery ranges.

Northwards is the great moorland area round the headwaters of the Rivers Teifi and Towy, which Giraldus called Ellenith. The highest point is Drygarn Fawr (2,115 feet) south of the new Claerwen Reservoir. The man-made lakes in the valleys of the Elan and the Claerwen, supplying water to Birmingham, flooded pastoral lands with farms and a mansion where Shelley once stayed. This was one of the earliest of the 'water supply landscapes', now fully accepted and possibly more scenically attractive than the lakeless valley it replaced. There were three dams in the original scheme, each around 500 feet long and 120 feet high, built at successive levels up the valley of the Elan and creating a chain of lakes seven miles long. The new Claerwen Dam, only completed in the last few years, is longer and higher and holds back an even bigger lake. These moors, once the waterworks are left behind, are still the most remote part of southern Britain, particularly towards the south-west where the Tregaron Bog, a waste of cotton grass, is a haunt of the polecat. The once narrow and adventurous road from Rhayader to Devil's Bridge with loose surface, steep hills and fords, is now metalled and used by motor coaches; cars also use the old drovers' road from Tregaron to Abergwesyn. Still an adventure, though not of the sort he found, is the crossing described by Cliffe from Llanddewi Brevi to Ystrad Ffin. This he did in the 1840s at the time of the Rebecca Insurrection, which starting with the possibly worthy aim of burning down toll-gates, spread soon to murder, robbery and general incendiarism. Cliffe ran into a band of 20 of the rioters, but taking them by surprise was past before they could harm him.

There is little hereabouts for the rock climber, though it is interesting to note that, while Haskett Smith pointed out long ago the possibilities of the Elan Valley, no climb was actually made there until the 1950s.

North of the main road to Aberystwyth rises Plynlimon Fawr (2,468 feet). Recently the Ordnance Survey decided that henceforward we must call it Plumlummon, reverting thus to an alternative spelling known also to George Borrow and which he translated as 'Five Points'; by now, however, the other has been in use for so long and is so familiar that we will continue with it here. This is one of the best-known of Welsh hills, specially notable as the source of the Severn and the Wye; Defoe thought it might be the highest hill in the country and compared it with the mountain in Switzerland which feeds on various sides the Rhine, the Rhone and the Aa. By the nineteenth century it was usual to be derogatory; thus Haskett Smith says:

> Plynlimon is seldom mentioned except with derision. The Beauties of Wales (1813) does indeed speak of 'the towering summit which bears the name of Plinlimmon', and quotes the equally appropriate description given by Philips
>
> > That cloud-piercing hill
> > Plinlimmon from afar the traveller kens,
> > Astonished how the goats their shrubby browse
> > Gnaw pendent.

But, in truth, the great difficulty which travellers have, whether far or near, is to ken it at all; and many of them have vented their disappointment in words of bitter scorn.

Pennant (1770) candidly admits that he never saw it, which is easily understood, for the mountain is neither easy to see nor worth looking at when seen. The ascent is a protracted bog-walk.

The ascent from Eisteddfa Gurig, the highest point of the Aberystwyth road, is ideal for children climbing their first mountain. A thousand feet of ascent and only 2½ miles of walking on a cart track followed by easy slopes with large stakes marking the way lead to a splendid viewpoint—near valleys and reservoirs, mile upon mile of hill-top of similar height and contour, the sea and, in the limit of the view, the real mountains of the Brecon Beacons, Cader Idris and the Arans. Recently a similarly easy way has become available from the new reservoir to the west. From the north, say from the Llyfnant Valley at Machynlleth, it is still a long hill tramp through the sort of featureless upland country which, being superficially dull enough to have to yourself, is for this reason completely delightful. Borrow crossed from Machynlleth to Pont Erwyd by way of the Potosi Lead Mine, then being actively worked. A few days later he returned to visit the summit of Plynlimon and the river sources, claiming in his book that this was the 'third in Wales for altitude, being only inferior to Snowdon and Cadair Idris'.

From Plynlimon the Wye flows south-eastwards and the Severn east, then north-east; they enclose between them a huge area of hill country which falls mostly in Radnorshire and a peculiar-shaped westward-jutting piece of Shropshire. Close to the Wye inside the big bend beyond Builth Wells, Gwaun Ceste Hill (1,778 feet) near the isolated village of Glascwm is the highest point in 100 square miles of hill country.

Radnor Forest is a compact hill block to the north of New Radnor; it is flat topped, the highest point, Great Rhos (2,166 feet), rising but little above the surrounding peat bogs. On the south side is the waterfall picturesquely called 'Water-Break-Its-Neck'. The northern slopes are newly afforested, providing terrain which is exceedingly hard to cross; forestry roads often contour the hill-sides and lead the traveller far out of his way, while to traverse the plantations is hard going and probably forbidden anyway.

Northwards the hills march on. There is one twisting major road from Newtown to Llandrindod Wells down the Ithon Valley, dividing this area from north to south and the odd secondary road such as that which follows the upper Teme Valley down to Knighton. Beyond the Teme the hill mass continues into Shropshire as Clun Forest, the far edge of which looks across to Corndon, the Stiperstones, the Long Mynd and England.

Between the Severn and the boundaries of the Snowdonia National Park the county of Montgomery presents us with similar hills all the way from Plynlimon, the summit of which is just in Cardiganshire, to the River Dee at Llangollen. Llyn Vyrnwy, one of Liverpool's water sources, is notably beautiful. Again away from the few roads this is indeed wild and lonely country. Beyond the Milltir Cerrig Pass, which carries the Llangynog to Bala road and which forms part of the eastern boundary of the Park, are the Berwyn Mountains, the highest point—Moel Sych (2,713 feet)—being shared between Montgomery and Denbigh. Cader Berwyn nearby on the same county boundary is only a foot lower. The south-eastern slopes are seamed by a series of steep-sided valleys in one of which, above Llanrhaiadr ym Mochnant, is Pistyll Rhaiadr, the highest waterfall in Wales.

Above Llangollen on the north side of the Dee is Dinas Bran, which Mackintosh calls 'the steepest conical mountain on all sides in South

Britain, though its height is not very great'. Actually it is about 1,000 feet. On top are fragments of a castle. Leland says of it: 'Ther bredith in the Rok Side that the Castelle stondith on every yere an Egle. And the Egle doth sorely assaut hym that distroith the Nest goyng down in one Basket and having an other over his Hedde to defend the sore Stripe of the Egle!' Haskett Smith quotes this as an early example of the use of the climbing rope and adds, 'Under such circumstances a climber ought to find St Paul a better patron saint than St Martin.'

The northern slopes of the valley of the Dee rise to 1,892 feet at Moel y Gamelin. Mountain Limestone outcrops in horizontal light-coloured bands on Eglwyseg Mountain and some climbing has been done there. Ruabon Mountain, nearby to the east, looks out over the coalfield to the Cheshire Plain. The Clwydian Range (Moel Fammau, 1,820 feet) runs alongside the broad and fertile Vale of Clwyd for some 20 miles on towards the northern coast. These hills are of older rocks but the limestone is never very far away, so that hereabouts is a minor caving area. Between the Clwyd and the Conway are the Denbighshire Moors—the Mynydd Hiraethog—a desolate heather-clad tract reaching 1,742 feet, with a road summit of 1,523 feet near the 'Sportsman's Arms'.

There are two further areas on the far side of the Park which can be most appropriately dealt with here. In the Lleyn Peninsula a compact hill group, the Rivals, rises almost direct from the sea to 1,849 feet. These steep northern slopes had been a prominent feature in the view from the Welsh mountains for many decades but it was not until the 1950s that climbers really came to look at them. They found much of interest, as well as something normally regarded as an Alpine hazard and unusual in this country. The path to the crags from the east passes below a stone tip from quarries high up on the hill, occasionally stones come all the way down whanging across the line of the path with all the venom of a high mountain stone fall. On one of the summits is Tre'r Ceiri, an ancient hill fort with circles of stone huts, in a commanding though surely waterless position. Anglesey has, perhaps, the lowest 'mountains' in the country. Holyhead Mountain, which Ruskin called 'a mighty granite rock beyond the moors of Anglesey, splendid in its heathery crest, a foot planted in the deep sea', is on the tip of

57

Holy Island and 720 feet. More prosaically it provides shelter for the cross-channel port. Parys Mountain, only 450 feet, is even smaller. It rises in the north-east corner of the island above Amlwch and has on its slopes copper mines worked since Roman times.

10 *The Climber's Way a*
the Nant Ffra

THREE

Snowdonia National Park

We now turn to the Snowdonia National Park, which we have already almost encircled. Here the rounded slopes, the uniform ranks of hills are left behind and we come at last to range upon range of real mountains, with steep sides and jagged crests, ice and frost worn. These are the remains of a large dome of arched beds which probably extended at one time to 20,000 feet above the present ground level. The hills near Snowdon and the Cader Idris range are corresponding outcrops of similar strata, the hills between are remnants of beds which are even older. The present-day Snowdonia National Park has an area of more than 800 square miles and incorporates most of the counties of Merioneth (except the north-east corner) and Caernarvon (only the Peninsulas of Lleyn and Great Orme are excluded), plus a corner of Denbigh. The Snowdon National Forest Park, the biggest section of which lies close to Betws-y-Coed, falls within this area. There are 14 peaks above 3,000 feet and some 150 more between 2,000 and 3,000 feet. The 14 have frequently been traversed in one continuous expedition. This started as a trip for walkers, taking 12 hours or so for the 30 miles with its 18,000 feet of ascent and descent. Then came what Samivel calls *L'Alpiniste Chronometre*—'*Ôtez-lui sa montre; il n'a plus d'impression*'—and this record time was beaten again and again. Finally cross-country runners took a hand and the most recent fast time (by E. Beard) is 5 hours 26 minutes, involving climbing and descending at the astonishing rates of 3,000 and 6,000 feet per hour respectively.

The mountains of Wales have been steeped in legend and romance since earliest times. Many of the Arthurian legends, collected together

Tryfan, Caernarvonshire   61

in the *Mabinogion*, can be sited hereabouts; for example King Arthur and his knights sleep in a cave near Lliwedd, the name of Merlin is linked with Dinas Emrys in Nant Gwynant, and so on. Geoffrey Young has drawn attention to the first recorded ascent of rock in Wales in the words of Sir Thomas Malory—'King Arthur yoed up to the creste of the cragge, and than he comforted himself with the colde winde'. 'Here', comments Young, 'are compressed all the elements that make up a good climb; its successful completion, the personal reaction of the climber, and his motive.'

The first traveller to leave an account was Giraldus (1188), who wrote—'On the highest parts of the mountains of Eryri are two lakes worthy of admiration. The one has a floating island in it, which is often driven from one side to the other by the force of the winds; and the shepherds behold with astonishment their cattle, whilst feeding, carried to distant parts of the lake . . . The other lake is noted for a wonderful and singular miracle. It contains three sorts of fish— eels, trout and perch, all of which have only one eye, the left being wanting.' (Reference is to Llyn y Dywarchen above Rhyd-ddu and Llyn y Cwn on the Glyders.)

Early in the sixteenth century Leland found this country much more wooded than it is today: 'The best wood of Caernarvonshire is by Glinne Kledder and by Glin Llughy and by Capel Kiryk and at Llan-peris. More upwarde be Eryri Hilles, and in them ys very little corne. If there were the Deere would destroy it.' And, as one might expect, he found the higher parts 'horrible with the sight of bare stones'.

Camden, in his *Brittania*, a topographical description of England and Wales written in Latin towards the end of the same century, dubbed these mountains 'the British Alps'—'Nature has here reared huge groups of mountains, as if she intended to bind fast the bowels of the earth . . . Here are so many crags and rocks, so many wooded valleys, so many lakes, that these mountains may be truly called the British Alps, for they are, like the Alps, bespread with broken crags on every side, all surrounding one (Snowdon), which, towering in the centre, far above the rest, lifts its head so loftily, as if it meant not only to threaten, but to thrust it into the sky'.

A hundred years later Camden was translated by Edward Lhwyd, who not only corrected inaccuracies but also added some attractive

Snowdonia National Park

new text in which he revealed a knowledge of the district much in advance of previous writers. We can still appreciate his simple exposition of mountain travel—'having climbed up one Rock, we come to a valley, and most commonly to a lake; and by passing that, we ascend another, and sometimes a third and a fourth, before we arrive at the highest Peaks'.

Prior to 1800 there were no roads through the mountains and those travellers that did come used only paths and trackways. Several left accounts of their journeys, the most interesting being Thomas Pennant, whose *Journey to Snowdon* was published in 1781. Described by Dr Johnson as 'the best traveller I have ever read', he climbed many of the local mountains and made precise records of what he saw. But soon the roads were to open up the country and more and more visitors came, first to walk and to sight-see, later to climb.

The mountains of the Park divide into a number of natural groups and these we will now consider in turn.

The Carnedds form an extensive upland area, ten miles across, between the sea coast, the Conway Valley and the Nant Ffrancon. Here are six of the 3,000-foot mountains—Carnedd Llewelyn (3,484 feet) and Carnedd Dafydd (3,426 feet), the second and third highest in Wales, as well as Pen yr Oleu Wen, Yr Elen, Foel Grach and Foel Fras. These are comparatively featureless hills with long wide slopes requiring careful compass work in a mist. The mightiest crag hereabouts is Craig yr Ysfa at the head of Cwm Eigiau. One November night in 1925 the small dam in this valley burst and spilled the contents of the lake down into the Conway. The village of Dolgarrog was overwhelmed and 16 lives were lost. Cwm Eigiau was the site of the first climbing hut in this country, set up by the Rucksack Club just before the 1914–18 War.

Jutting out into the sea on the north side of the group is the bulky headland of Penmaenmawr, for a long time a great obstacle to travellers to Ireland. The Romans avoided it by a high pass inland, the Bwlch y Ddeufaen; later a path was beaten out round the seaward flanks of the Head, said in the reign of James I to be a yard wide and cut in the face of the rock 600 feet above the sea. John Wesley in 1756 said of it— 'the road runs so far above the beach that one could not venture to look down, but that there is a wall built all along, about four feet high.

Meantime, the ragged cliff hangs over one's head, as if it would fall every moment'. But by 1774 Dr Johnson found 'a way lately made very easy and very safe. It is cut smooth, and enclosed between parallel walls, the outer of which secures the passenger from the precipice, which is deep and dreadful. The inner wall preserves the road from loose stones, which the shattered steep above it would pour down.' Subsequently there were frequent troubles from stone falls and finally the present highway was engineered with tunnels at the steepest places.

There is, of course, little or no record of who first climbed mountains like these. We know, for instance, that Thomas Johnson, the botanist, reached nearly to the top of Carnedd Llewelyn in 1639, turning back only because his guide was afraid of eagles. Because it was the highest Snowdon was climbed by many subsequent visitors, but the lesser mountains by comparison hardly at all. Occasionally there were scares that Carnedd Llewelyn was the higher, such as the ascent noted in *Phil. Trans.* in 1771, 'which satisfied the climber and his water level that the summit was higher than that of Snowdon'. Pennant a few years later drew the opposite conclusion from a similar observation. The order of precedence was finally settled in favour of Snowdon towards the end of the nineteenth century. As Haskett Smith puts it— 'to have reduced Snowdon would have been a real misfortune, as the old-established favourite is beyond all question the finer mountain of the two. Only imagine the feelings of a poor peak abandoned in its old age, without cheap trippers, without huts, without a railway, without Sir Edward Watkin. The blow would have been too cruel!'

The Nant Ffrancon which forms the southern and western boundaries of the Carnedds has some curious features. The highest point is close to the foot of Tryfan and here Telford's road actually forms the watershed—a stream on one side flows to Ogwen and the sea near Bangor, while one on the other flows to the Llugwy and the sea at Conway. The Ogwen passes westwards through Llyn Ogwen and then tumbles down the Benclog Falls into a wide flat-bottomed valley at right angles to its former course. This valley was carved out by a glacier flowing northwards off the Glyders and the hanging valleys left behind as the ice cut down are prominent on the western slopes. A century and a half ago, we are told, these cwms were the summer leys of horned cattle and mountain horses, while the surrounding cliffs were inhabited by sheep and goats. There was at one time a lake, three miles long, in the floor of the main valley, but this subsequently silted up. Lower down above Bethesda is one of the major slate quarries of the area.

Nant Ffrancon has been translated as the 'Valley of Beavers', but the derivation offered to Borrow when he passed this way in 1854 was quite different—'Nant yr Ieuanc gwn, the Pass of the Young Dogs, because when one shouts it answers with a noise resembling the crying of hounds'. Rather than look at his surroundings, Borrow preferred to talk to people. He noted the craggy Gallt yr Ogof and the cottage, now the Climbers' Club Hut, 'a wretched hovel', but falling in with a talkative carpenter his account makes no further reference to mountains. Thirty years before the author of *Pleasure Tours* did not miss anything when passing this way:

> The fantastic piles of rock, which compose the sides, rise abruptly from the base, and stretch their barren points to the clouds. Sometimes part of these impending cliffs, when undermined, give way, and fall down in immense masses, in their passage dislodging thousands of other stones, until the whole becomes as if one universal ruin. The mountains at the upper end of this vale form a scene singularly grand; on each side the hollow appears guarded by huge conical rocks, with some mountains at a distance to shut up the vale; the whole forming a scene of the most imposing kind.

On the far side rises the ridge of the Glyders stretching southwards from Elidyr Fawr (3,029 feet) between Llanberis and Bethesda to Y Garn (3,104 feet), and Glyder Fawr (3,269 feet), then turning abruptly east to Glyder Fach (3,262 feet) and on towards Capel Curig. In the bend in the range and 200 feet above Llyn Ogwen is the hollow of Cwm Idwal, cradling the sombre waters of Llyn Idwal and edged by the great crags of Idwal Slabs, Glyder Fawr and the Devil's Kitchen Cliff. In the centre of the latter is the famous black cleft from which the crag gets its name—a good setting this time for association with the devil. An active scrambler can penetrate the floor for some distance, as Cliffe did in 1843, but only the expert climber can pass this way to the plateau above. The summit of Glyder Fach is notably rocky, a chaos in fact of jammed boulders, said by the bard Taliesin to be the grave of the warrior Ebediw. Many travellers feel they can detect the hand of man among these summit rocks, Cliffe for instance:

The scene before us, in fact, resembled the ruins of some vast Druidical temple—a mountain Stonehenge—which had been overthrown ages ago by some awful convulsion of nature. Indeed, so strong was our impression that we were in the midst of venerable Druidical remains, that it was some time ere we could convince ourselves that what we saw was in reality a chaotic mass of stones thrown into inconceivable confusion—the work of time and the violence of the elements.

From Glyder Fach the aptly named Bristly Ridge runs down northwards to the col of Bwlch Tryfan, behind which rises the famous cocked-hat-shaped Tryfan (3,010 feet), 'the three headed mountain'. When viewed end-on from the upper slopes of the Carnedds opposite, this appears conical and remarkably steep. The craggy east face is a wonderful playground for moderate climbers and is thoroughly nail-scratched. Two rock pillars on the summit, often mistaken for humans by travellers on the road below, are in fact about ten feet high and offer an exciting jump from one to the other. Haskett Smith says of them:

> Large as the pillars are it is difficult to believe that they were placed in the position they occupy by unassisted nature; they seem too upright, too well squared, and too level-topped; with a cross-piece on the top they would form a nobly placed 'trilithon', of which any 'dolmen-builder' would be proud.

There are several famous crags on the northern slopes of the range and they offer great variations in rock type and structure. On Tryfan holds are large and satisfying, on Glyder Fach the rock is notably rough but on Idwal Slabs it is much smoother, while around the Devil's Kitchen lush vegetation grows in cracks and on ledges; all these lend variety to local rock work.

The Llanberis Pass separating the Glyders from the Snowdon Group is narrow, steep-sided and impressive. There are massive crags on either hand and spectators watching the climbers at work cause traffic jams on the road below. Signs of glacial action are plentiful. A road, first built about 1830, climbs through it from Llanberis with its lakes, slate quarries and castle to the Pen-y-Pass Hotel at 1,169 feet and continues down the other side to the equally well known Pen-y-Gwryd Hotel at the head of Nant Gwynant. Both these have taken their turn at various times as centre of the local mountaineering world. Above Pen-y-Pass towers the fine conical peak of Crib Goch, connected by the wall-like Crib Goch Ridge to the main mountain mass behind. This is the line of the famous Snowdon Horseshoe walk, which continues round Cwm Dyli over the main peak of Snowdon to the summit of Lliwedd opposite.

Y Wyddfa (3,560 feet) is the highest point of the Snowdon Group and, indeed, anywhere in these islands south of mid-Scotland. It is a shapely peak, effectively buttressed on various sides by its satellites—Lliwedd, Crib Goch, Crib y Ddysgl and Yr Aran. The layout of the whole is best seen from Capel Curig over the Llynau Mymbyr, but the main peak impresses most where it towers above Cwm y Llan or Cwm Dyli. Snowdon is a popular ascent and there are several well-marked paths, all perfectly easy in clear weather in the summer, and also a mountain railway to take travellers to the summit. The principal routes are from Llanberis by the long north ridge over Crib y Ddysgl, from Pen-y-Pass by Cwm Dyli (the Pig Track), from Beddgelert through Cwm y Llan (the Watkin Path) or starting from points on the Caernarvon road, and from Snowdon Ranger along the top of Clogwyn Du'r Arddu. The finest precipices are in Cwm Dyli below the summit, the face of Lliwedd above Llyn Llydaw and Clogwyn Du'r Arddu. In the winter conditions may be vastly different; if the easy paths of the summit are iced over, only mountaineers experienced in dealing with snow and ice and suitably equipped and clad can safely tackle these various ways. The rack railway which runs from Llanberis employs the double-cog Abt System similar to that of the Gornergrat and Pike's Peak Railways. Since it was opened in January, 1896, large numbers of people have reached the top this way and many a lost and mist-bewildered party has been glad to follow the lines downhill to safety.

One of the first recorded ascents of the mountain, though there must have been others previously, was made by the botanist Thomas Johnson in 1639, when 20 plants were collected and listed. Snowdon remained the lodestone for all adventurous travellers in the years that followed. Two hundred years later Cliffe noted that 200 to 300 visitors a day were reaching the summit from Llanberis in the height of the season, adding—'from this it will appear that the romance of the ascent of Snowdon belongs to the past', words which are even more true today. The summit hotel had just been erected and 'tea, coffee, ale, porter, spirits and other refreshments' could be obtained. Many travellers took guides:

> The charge for ponies is the same at all inns; viz. five shillings to the summit, if practicable; but, if you proceed over the mountain—say, for instance, from Beddgelert to Llanberis—the charge is then doubled. The guides' fees vary. From Beddgelert, the guides charge seven shillings to the summit; if afterwards they proceed with a party to Llanberis or Pen-y-Gwyrd, the fee is ten shillings; sometimes, when there is a large party, a higher sum is voluntarily paid. A night ascent to Snowdon from Beddgelert is ten shillings, which is moderate enough. The expense of a guide from Pen-y-Gwryd—a much more fatiguing ascent, and nearly the same distance—is only five shillings. Llanberis is far in advance on the score of cheapness. When a large party join together, as is almost always the case, the guides' fee for a single individual is a mere trifle. The charge from Snowdon Ranger is about the same as Beddgelert. From Capel Curig, which is a great deal the longest journey, the guides' charge is ten shillings.

In terms of today's values these were large sums.

Borrow, though describing Snowdon as 'one of the most celebrated hills of the world and to poets of modern Europe almost what Parnassus was to those of old' spent his time on the summit airing his knowledge of Welsh and apologizing for being English.

Otherwise, from the long and varied history of Snowdon we only have room for one or two bizarre points. David Hewitt of Beddgelert is said to have climbed the mountain 580 times. P. S. Minor, who had already been up 87 times, once spent three weeks at Rhyd-ddu during which time he climbed it another 19 times. During the last war a soldier from the Mountain Training Wing at Llanberis ran from there to the summit in 48 minutes and down again in 26.

Beyond the Caernarvon–Beddgelert road the western hills are grouped in the shape of a letter T with the bar parallel to the road. To the south above Beddgelert is Moel Hebog, 'the hill of the hawk', and to the north the massive Mynydd Mawr, where the great crag of Castell Cidwm rising from Llyn Cwellyn reminded Borrow of Gibraltar. The stroke of the T runs westwards from Y Garn to Carnedd Goch above Nantlle. The weather here is reputed to be better than in the higher mountains farther east and climbers are recommended to visit Craig Cwm Silin, with its Great Slab, when conditions at Ogwen are too miserable. These are the last big mountains in this direction and they overlook the Lleyn Peninsula and large stretches of sea.

South Snowdon is the name given by climbers to the block of mountains bordered by Nant Gwynant, the Rivers Llugwy and Conway, the Vale of Ffestiniog and the Aberglaslyn Pass, the highest point of which is the extensive Moel Siabod (2,860 feet) above Capel Curig. At the western end is Moelwyn, beneath which lies the ugly slate district of Blaenau Ffestiniog, and Cnicht (2,265 feet), the Welsh Matterhorn, remarkably steep from some viewpoints but in reality an elongated cocked-hat.

The Rhinogs, the main ridge of which runs parallel to the coast behind Harlech, are worthy hills, though they reach only to 2,475 feet at Llethr. These are older rocks than those north and south, sharp-edged, slaty types with abundant heather. The Roman Steps, a flagged pathway climbing from Llyn Cwm Bychan to a pass over the range was probably a mediaeval pack-way; now by a curious progress it leads down to the Atomic Power Station at Trawsfynydd. Eastwards towards Bala is an immense tract of wild and little-visited mountain country. The highest peak is Arenig Fawr (2,800 feet) which, rising impressively above the Bala-Ffestiniog road, forces itself on the notice of travellers like, for example, Borrow, who found 'something majestic in its huge bulk. Of all the hills which I saw in Wales none made a greater impression on me'. This was the site of one of our earliest meteorological stations, for rainfall experiments carried out here by the Hon. Daines Barrington were described in *Phil. Trans.* in 1773. Farther south Rhobell Fawr stands in shapeless isolation above the valley of the upper Mawddach.

The Cader Idris range, the southern rim of the great eroded dome, runs parallel to the Mawddach Estuary on the south side from Barmouth to Dolgellau. The northern face is everywhere steep or craggy—'the walls of Dolgellau', it has been said, 'are three miles high'. Defoe, as often, found the mountains hereabouts impassable—'we looked at them indeed with astonishment for their rugged tops and the immense height of them. Some are of the opinion', he added, 'that Kader

Idricks is the highest mountain in Wales'. The name means 'Chair of Idris'; Idris was a giant who must have found the 2,927-foot summit a magnificent resting place, even if somewhat cold and damp. As will be seen in due course, a significant contribution to British rock climbing was made in 1888 on the face of this mountain above the Foxes Path. A few years later an accident on the same climb was to have a profound influence on yet another sport; Arnold Lunn, who badly injured a leg in a fall here, was forced to concentrate thenceforward on ski-ing, a sport which he revolutionized in subsequent years.

The last group in the Snowdon Park rises beyond Bwlch Oerddrws, 'the cold door', south of the upper Dee Valley. Aran Mawddwy (2,970 feet) is the highest mountain in Merioneth and, indeed, in Wales south of Snowdon. Aran Benllyn nearby is only a few feet lower. The northern slopes are gentle and can be climbed almost anywhere, those to the south are steep and craggy, though except at Cwm Cowarch above Dinas Mawddwy not sufficiently so to please the rock climber. Drayton mentions these hills in *Polyolbion*:

> *With very sweet Cader Idric did drop*
> *And mighty Raran shook his proud sun-kissing top.*

His outlook seems a good deal more modern than Defoe's.

From the Arans we can look out into central Wales, to the Berwyns, the Montgomeryshire hills and Plynlimon, all of them outside the bounds of the Park, and beyond them to the mountains of South Wales.

We have seen how, during the nineteenth century, many travellers came to the Welsh hills, climbing not only Snowdon, which had always been a popular ascent, but others of the surrounding heights also. While most of them stuck to paths, took local guides and only climbed in the fairest of weather, others adventured into all sorts of wild places in the course of their climbs. Typical of the latter was the 'climbing parson' who, as Cliffe tells us, used to follow the skyline of every mountain he visited and 'no rocks, however rough, no precipices— unless perfectly inaccessible—ever daunted him . . . Picture to yourself a tall man, about fifty-two years of age, of a wiry, spare habit, rather slightly built, dressed in a pair of dingy slop trousers, a linen spencer of the same complexion, without hat or covering of any sort for the head, no neck-tie, his shirt collar unbuttoned, with an enormous Alpenstock or climbing pole, seven or eight feet in length in his hand, and you may perhaps be able to form some idea of him'.

Men like this were the forerunners. Then came the Alpine climbers, parties of whom began to rendezvous at Pen-y-Gwryd in the 1870s. They spent winter and spring holidays here and notes of their activities sometimes found their way into the *Alpine Journal*.

In 1882, the year in which (as we shall see later) W. P. Haskett Smith was engaged in his first big climbing campaign in the Lake District, T. W. Wall and A. H. Stocker made the first real climb in North Wales on the great face of Lliwedd. These were experienced Alpine mountaineers who felt that here they were attacking an Alpine-type problem. The first gully climb, of what had by then become the Lake District model, took place on Tryfan in 1887. Soon afterwards an outstanding event took place farther south when Owen Glynne Jones, a young Londoner with family ties in Barmouth, came to spend his holidays in that little seaside town with its marvellous view of Cader Idris. This attracted him strongly. Though obviously acquainted with some of the classics of Alpine literature, he had no knowledge of contemporary climbing either in the north round Snowdon or in the Lake District. When, therefore, in 1888 he made a rock climb on the face of Cader Idris, it was done entirely on his own initiative, so that we have to class him, with J. W. Puttrell on gritstone and W. P. Haskett Smith in Cumberland, as one of the founders of British rock climbing. Jones did most of his subsequent climbing in the Lake District, but years later when he brought his young friends, the Abraham brothers, to look over his home mountains, here is how one of them described it:

> Our route brought us out on the grassy ledge which leads into the gully here. A fine waterfall, about thirty feet in height, splashed across it, and we pretended to take for granted that the continuation of our climb lay up to the right of this. Jones soon undeceived us. He intended to try and keep in the bed of the gully, to climb the waterfall in fact, and despite our most piteous appeals he would not waver in his decision. Our only hope of avoiding a good soaking lay in his not being able to get up. Buttoning up his coat, he plunged through the water to the back of the pitch and slowly struggled upwards, we below anxiously awaiting the outcome of his

exertions and shivering as we saw dimly, through the curtain of water, his lithe body, like some huge amphibian, slowly ascending.

He got on swimmingly, in more ways than one, and was soon under the crest of the pitch. Now came the crux. The water was here concentrated in a solid jet which poured over with considerable impetus. His position was one of such discomfort as would not allow of his keeping us long in suspense. Was it in too much force for him? He commenced to traverse out, and thrust his hand through the water to grasp a handhold on the right wall. Then he pulled his body forward, and the water struck him full on top of the head, splashing off it, fan-like, on to the walls of the gully. He was quite blinded, progress was impossible, and after stoically standing its battering until fatigued, he withdrew into the shelter of the chockstone— amid our cheers!

He evinced no desire for another attempt, but came down hand over hand and out through the water, quite exhausted with the strain. We stripped him and wrung out his wet garments, whilst the amateur photographer of the party exposed his only plate on us.

Truly these Victorians climbed for the fun of it!

The first outstanding climber in Wales was J. M. A. Thomson, a schoolmaster from Llandudno; he started to climb early in the 1890s and continued to dominate the scene until his death in 1912. O. G. Jones did come in 1898 with the Abraham brothers bent on writing a companion volume to his Lake District book, but in the following year he was killed in the Alps. The Abrahams continued their visits after the death of Jones and they finally produced in 1906 the book on Welsh climbing which he had planned. Thomson began his climbing in gullies, then gradually expanded his technique until he was making much harder lines on slabs and walls; progress in this respect paralleled that in the Lake District. He was a taciturn man who, though he wrote but little, had an individual literary style:

The accommodation on the ledge was scanty; neither a sitting or a standing posture gave the requisite security, but a trial of the former revealed the existence of a singularly sharp spike of rock hidden in a tuft of heather. With feet below and arms upon the ledge I could now play the rope round the pointed spillikin. The second man came up unfalteringly. The next move was made along a vein of quartz which soon lost itself in a buttress set with overhanging projections, and presenting a seemingly impassable barrier. A direct assault upon the rocks on the east side was the only alternative to retreat. They receded but little from the vertical, and the difficulty was accentuated at a point where it became necessary to make a stride of abnormal length, and while at full stretch in an exposed position, with one handhold for a mainstay, swing the weight across on to the right foot. About fifty feet from the last anchorage I reached the semblance of a niche, and seated here on a solitary grass tuft, with the rope drawn tight over a solid bollard of rock, could await my companion with the utmost composure of mind. In response to enquiries as to what was to be done next, I could only guess the position of my companion and extol the true-fixed quality of the high hold for the right hand. Soon after I caught sight of a hat a few feet below me. The nook is one of those from which each newcomer must necessarily evict the man already established, so, having no alternative, I exchanged the seat on the eyrie for a stance on the belaying-bitt. From this aerial spot the view was unique. I seemed to be standing on a vertebra of the backbone of the mountain. An impossible crag rose directly above, and smooth slabs shelving away on either side presented an outline of delicately undulating curves. This romantic environment produces on the mind an impression of isolation at a great height.

Climbing had become much less of a prank, much more of a cult, and was developing both jargon and traditions.

In Wales the 1914–18 War made a serious break in the story and afterwards, while Lake District climbing expanded buoyantly, that of Wales took a decade to recover. When the revival did come, it was another schoolmaster, H. R. C. Carr, who was the outstanding personality. Climbing was still a gay and light-hearted activity, as we gather from Carr's own writing:

Forty feet higher is the second overhanging chimney which runs up directly to the base of the Nose. Here there is a ledge charmingly situated. Peering hopefully round the base of the Nose, the leader discerns an attractive line of advance on its southern side. A series of steps and an angle-crack conduct him to a sloping stance on a vertical wall with the third overhanging chimney out of reach on his right. Hold is provided for the feet, but for a moment there appears to be nothing very suitable for the hands. Calling loudly upon the patron saint of the locality, the leader explores the smooth and vertical face with eager fingers. The saint, responsive to so urgent a request, opens a cunning little cavity in the rock precisely where it is least expected and most desired. The thankful climber is now able to swing boldly across the wall and quickly gains the security of the chimney.

But harder and grimmer times were ahead. In 1929 two new, enterprising and very diverse characters came on the scene; both were from Liverpool, which these days provides heroes for youth in a quite different field. The first of them, Colin Kirkus, extended within the next few years the limits of what was possible on British rocks, bringing a new order of courage into climbing. On his routes stances were farther apart, as much as 120 to 150 feet, so that the second could do little for the leader if he fell, while the lengthy pitches of hard climbing meant protracted periods of mental tension for the leader—the long frail rope his only connection with the world of man. The great crag of Clogwyn Du'r Arddu was opened up and new climbs were made on the steeper parts of most others. Here is Kirkus in action, described by A. B. Hargreaves:

> With some difficulty my leader got himself lodged in a sort of saint's niche about 20–25 feet up and then proceeded to fix the piton in a crack at the back. This was not so easy because he had to hold himself into the niche with one hand while hammering the piton with the other. However, he eventually got it in to his satisfaction, then he ran his rope through the ring and climbed down for a rest. We both pulled hard on the rope and the piton was O.K.'d as firm. Then Colin went at the pitch. His idea was to use the rope running through the piton to hold him in while he leaned back and reached upwards for the holds which he hoped existed above the overhang. He tried once—and came back into the niche—he tried again (harder) with me holding the rope taut—and then—(a loud 'ping' and a 'whirr')—the piton was out and Colin was in mid-air . . . Fortunately, although the Bilberry Terrace from which we were operating was quite broad at that point, I had a belay, though rather a small one, and was able to get some rope in during his gracefully parabolic descent, because he landed on his stomach at the very edge of the Terrace and just as the rope came tight on him he bounced over the top of the Direct Start crack . . . The brakes held, but only after I had been dragged several feet with the belay rope (line) stretching like elastic. I can still see his legs waving in the air.

The second of the new climbers was J. Menlove Edwards whose major contribution was the opening up of certain specialized crags, formerly shunned because the rock was poor and carried too much grass, heather and even trees. Both Kirkus and Edwards developed their skills on Cheshire sandstone at Helsby, but, after the second World War, the scene was dominated once again by gritstone climbers, first by P. R. J. Harding and A. J. J. Moulam, later by J. Brown, D. Whillans and others in the Rock and Ice Club. The latter group in particular covered Clogwyn Du'r Arddu with a network of routes, which for some time no one else could manage to repeat. Now standards are forging ahead again all round and several leaders can do all the very hardest of the climbs. Here is a present-day expert (J. A. Austin) at work; this writing can only give a true impression of the place to another top-grade climber; most of us could not even leave the ground on a route of this standard:

> The position here and for the next twenty feet was exacting, to say the least. The Ochre Slab has no bottom to it, and below it are overhanging walls and arêtes. This is not just a case of the buttress being a little out of plumb; the slab must be ten or twelve feet out beyond the foot of the cliff, and still above the left shoulder is a viciously overhanging wall, a slanting ceiling, which forms a bulge round which, a bit higher, one must layback. The climbing is exhilarating at this point, bold yet safe, and in a position which I am sure is unsurpassed in Wales. Round the bulge I went, to be faced by a very bold move, just at a time when I was certainly not feeling bold. The move consisted of lobbing a foot out sideways on to an angle on the sharp-edged rib on the right and pushing across on to it. I lobbed out, pushed and teetered into balance, then moved backwards across the groove to a good foothold above the band of overhangs. There is nothing to see from here but a few trees, the road and a couple of spectators in the field opposite. The path one has trodden is completely hidden under these massive bulges. The stance is not far away, and with some delicate use of a not too well placed piton I arrived. The word stance conjures up a vision of ledges, of walls less than vertical, of belays and room to stretch and to stand in comfort. This is none of those things, but a sort of nest-hole where it is possible to wedge in with head bent against the roof, feet splayed out on sloping flakes and a couple of well-placed pitons in the back to fasten one in.

Nowadays, generally speaking, the crags accessible from the Nant Ffrancon provide the easier straightforward climbs for moderate performers, those around the Llanberis Valley the harder climbs for the more expert. The great Lliwedd, Mecca for the greatest until the 1930s, is now largely neglected in favour of harder and more accessible places. Only exceptional leaders can discover and climb new lines in these specialist days; anyone else who fancies pioneering must go further afield, where crags are lower, more remote, and possibly of poorer quality rock. All routes have been minutely described in guidebooks and the difficulties can be assessed from the armchair before setting foot in the hills. The 'trade routes' have been blazoned for ever by the nailed boots of the past, the holds scratched and worn smooth; the rubber-soled boot came too late to save us from these trail marks. Throughout the summer and at week-ends all the year round hundreds of climbers and walkers camp on and climb over the most popular peaks; it becomes increasingly difficult to get the hills to oneself.

There are club huts specially built or adapted from cottages or barns; professional guides are available to lead novice or expert; in fact there are several ways by which the beginner can learn to climb safely and competently. There is an emphasis now on the teaching of technique. Experimenting goes on to improve equipment and methods and the results are dispersed widely through the climbing world. The whole atmosphere is purposeful and, even if one sighs occasionally for 'the good old days' when it required some determination to break into the world of climbing, it can be argued that the present highly organized community is in fact the only way to deal with the ever increasing volume of enthusiasts.

FOUR

The Backbone
of England

The Peak District, which falls mainly in Derbyshire, was the first National Park in the country, designated as such in 1950 and an obvious choice since half the population of England lives within 70 miles. Defoe called it 'the most desolate, wild and abandoned country in all England'; wild and desolate it remains, but it is abandoned no longer. The National Park area is 542 square miles, of which 160 are so-called 'water supply landscape'—reservoirs submerging farms and even villages, conifer plantations and access restrictions. 'The Peak' is a misnomer as the highest parts are not peaks at all but somewhat featureless elevated plateaux of moorland country. The word was derived in fact from Peac-land, the country of the ancient Peacs; this became Peakland and finally in the hands of those who did not understand the derivation, 'The Peak'.

The area is divisible into two, the Black, or High Peak in the north, peat moorland covered with heather and cotton grass where the rock is predominantly gritstone, and the White, or Low Peak in the south, Mountain Limestone country with light coloured rock and bright vegetation. Kinder Scout (2,088 feet) is the highest point, but Bleaklow on the other side of Longdendale is only a few feet lower. Kinder top, with something like six square miles above 2,000 feet is an extensive area of relatively flat peat bog dissected by drainage channels known as groughs. The surrounding country can only be seen from the edges giving a special feeling of remoteness to the centre of the plateau. As one North Country climber (John Wilding) has put it: 'Sometimes when standing in the centre of the plateau, under favourable atmospheric conditions, with the horizon falling on every side, and no ground within our vision higher than the curving lines of the moor immediately around us, one experiences that exhilarating sense of being actually on the roof of the world better than when standing on the summit of a high peak.' ·

A brief glance at the geology of the district helps us to understand the distribution of the various rocks. The gritstone strata, comprising four separate beds, lie uppermost; beneath them is a broad band of shale and the whole rests on a base of Mountain Limestone; all these have been folded into a ridge or dome. In places the upper parts of this ridge have been eroded away especially in the south where the whole thing is overlain with newer rocks. The result is that the High Peak has a capping of gritstone with the shales and limestones exposed in the valleys, while as we go southwards the gritstone thins out to narrow bands on either side of a broad limestone area. The gritstone is harder than the shale, so that as the latter wears away, the grit is left in steep cliffs above, called Edges. The most prominent of these are found round the Kinder, Bleaklow and Chew Moors plateaux and in an almost continuous line down the eastern edge of the district above the River Derwent—in succession, Bamford, Stanage, Burbage, Froggatt, Curbar, Baslow, Gardom's and Chatsworth Edges. Long sections take the form of rock walls 30 to 80 feet high and look from the valley like fortifications round the rims of the hills. The rock is a dirty brown colour, the corners and ledges are rounded and roofs and overhangs abound. It is unbelievably rough, sometimes like coarse sandpaper, sometimes studded with large sharp-edged crystals; all flat places, however small, have been scored by generations of nailed boots. The rock has been worked in the past for mill-stones, notably at Mill-stone Edge near Stanage, and giant wheels can still be found at some places forlornly buried in the base vegetation. Streams off the gritstone carve channels in the shales called cloughs. The only considerable waterfall is Kinder Downfall on the edge of the Kinder plateau above Hayfield. Periodically the shale is worn away to such an extent that a portion of the gritstone edge collapses on top of it, as at Alport Castles on Bleaklow; the face of the shale beds is exposed at Mam Tor, the Shivering Mountain, near Castleton. Finally where the streams run off the other rocks on to the limestone, caves are often found; some of the best-known show caves in the country are in the Peak District.

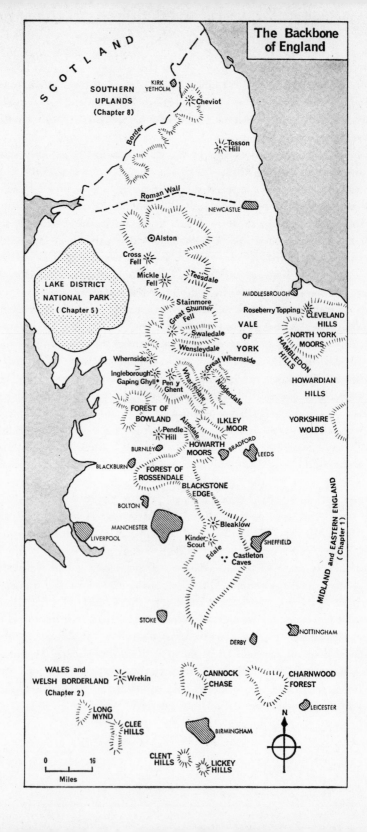

The Backbone of England

SCOTLAND

SOUTHERN UPLANDS (Chapter 8)

KIRK YETHOLM

Cheviot

Border

Tosson Hill

Roman Wall

NEWCASTLE

Alston

Cross Fell

Mickle Fell

Teesdale

MIDDLESBROUGH

Stainmore

Great Shunner Fell

Roseberry Topping

CLEVELAND HILLS

LAKE DISTRICT NATIONAL PARK (Chapter 5)

Swaledale

Wensleydale

VALE OF YORK

NORTH YORK MOORS

HAMBLEDON HILLS

Whernside

Great Whernside

Ingleborough

Gaping Ghyll

Pen y Ghent

Wharfedale

Nidderdale

HOWARDIAN HILLS

FOREST OF BOWLAND

Airedale

ILKLEY MOOR

YORKSHIRE WOLDS

Pendle Hill

BURNLEY

HOWARTH MOORS

BRADFORD

LEEDS

BLACKBURN

FOREST OF ROSSENDALE

BLACKSTONE EDGE

BOLTON

MANCHESTER

Bleaklow

LIVERPOOL

Kinder Scout

SHEFFIELD

Edale

Castleton Caves

MIDLAND and EASTERN ENGLAND (Chapter 1)

STOKE

NOTTINGHAM

DERBY

WALES and WELSH BORDERLAND (Chapter 2)

Wrekin

CANNOCK CHASE

CHARNWOOD FOREST

LEICESTER

LONG MYND

CLEE HILLS

BIRMINGHAM

N

CLENT HILLS

LICKEY HILLS

0 16

Miles

The hills and dales of the Peak have played a prominent part in the development of the sports of rock climbing, hill walking and caving in this country. The pioneer rock climber was J. W. Puttrell who went out from Sheffield to climb at Wharncliffe as long ago as 1888. As he had no contact until much later on with the march of events in either Wales or the Lake District, he can truly be regarded as an innovator in his own right, ranking thereby in the annals of the sport with W. P. Haskett Smith and O. G. Jones. In a year or two others joined him and soon the exploration was in full swing; climbs were made and records kept, culminating in the first guidebook by J. Laycock which appeared in 1913. The influence of gritstone has continued right up to the present day and, with only a few exceptions, all outstanding climbers in the Midlands and the North have practised their skills extensively on the edges of Peakland. Here they can discover the limits of their powers under fairly controllable conditions, as climbs can be tried with the safeguard of a rope held at the top by a companion. The friction properties of the rock are excellent and, as there are but few letterbox shaped holds, the gritstone climber soon develops the art of using sloping rounded holds, or holds made by jamming in rounded cracks, for both hands and feet. Nowadays large numbers of young people come out on these rocks every week-end; thorough exploration has produced thousands of climbs, now painstakingly listed in guidebooks, and standards are high indeed.

During the last decade climbing on the Mountain Limestone has become increasingly popular. Formerly this rock was regarded as unsafe for climbing—poor quality material outcropping in formidably steep faces, and it was only used to a limited extent by the pioneers. Such places were certainly being climbed on the Continent from the mid-1930s onwards by so-called artificial tactics, in which the leader is helped in the surmounting of difficulties by direct aid from his companions and in which free use is made of pitons (iron spikes) to provide holds where they are lacking. More of this later. These tactics were used increasingly in post-war years both on the Continent and in America and British climbers looking around for similar practice grounds in this country were attracted immediately to the great limestone crags of the Pennines. Climbs have been made on High Tor, Matlock, in Dovedale and the Manifold Valley, on several crags in the valley of the River Wye, south-east of Buxton, and elsewhere; there is now a climber's guidebook.

Close to Castleton there are several notable caverns, four of them open to the public. As Conan Doyle once wrote: 'All this country is hollow. Could you strike it with some gigantic hammer it would boom like a drum or possibly cave in altogether.' The most spectacular cave, at any rate as seen from the surface, is Peak Cavern below Peak Castle. This has an entrance 60 feet high at the foot of a vertical limestone crag, which leads to two-thirds of a mile of passages; the early part, where the public goes, is well lit and cared for but further in progress can only be made by crawls, squeezes and so on. Drayton quotes an unusual 'Devil' name for this cave; this shocked Defoe who only printed the first and last letters, taking pains to point out how inappropriate it was. For that matter all 'Devil' names are inappropriate anyway! Farther up the valley is Speedwell Cavern, where visitors make part of the trip by boat. They eventually reach the top of the Bottomless Pit, which is in fact 93 feet deep. Running westwards from Speedwell is the Winnats, an impressive limestone gorge reminiscent of Cheddar, with some smaller caves and some limestone rock climbs. On towards Mam Tor is Treak Cliff Cavern, at one time a notable source of the mineral fluorspar known hereabouts as Blue John; then finally highest up the valley is the Blue John Mine, not apparently in spite of its name as noted for the mineral as was Treak Cliff. These are of course all natural caves, but they might have remained for ever unpenetrated had it not been for the tunnelling activities of the ancient miners. There are other caves in the great limestone valleys farther south—Dovedale, Manifold, etc., and show caves at Matlock and Buxton. The only genuine pot-holes in the area, that is, vertical shafts similar to Gaping Ghyll in Yorkshire, are Eldon Hole and Nettle Pot. The former, at one time thought to be bottomless and the entrance to the 'infernal regions', was explored by J. Lloyd, F.R.S., in 1700 and found to be 180 feet deep. A depth of 525 feet has been reached, however, in recent years in Nettle.

Compared with walking, rock climbing and caving are specialist sports, both requiring to some degree physical fitness, technical ability and drive, both mental and physical. Walking on the other hand embraces a much wider range of activity from the gentlest of ambles to the toughest of struggles demanding all the above qualities in full measure. The walker moreover has all manner of things to divert him along the way, from birds and flowers and landscapes to the hands of his stopwatch. The walking aspects of any countryside as diverse as that of the Peak can be said, therefore, to mean much more to many more people than any of the other hill sports. In the last hundred years large numbers of young men and women from the surrounding towns have walked up and over these slopes to see what lies on the other side and have watched the changing moods of the valleys from the hills and of the hills from the valleys. With many square miles of strictly private moorland and the large number of potential visitors, Derbyshire has often been the scene of struggles over public rights-of-way, preservation of amenities and so forth. Feelings have at times run high, culminating in the Mass Trespass on Kinder Scout in 1932, as a result of which six walkers received prison sentences. Nowadays things are under better control from every point of view, though it is said that vandalism and hooliganism have increased since the Park was founded, as many believe that the 'National' signifies that the land belongs to the nation and thus to every one of them.

Alongside all the local developments in rock climbing then there grew up the parallel pursuit of hard walking; some was done by climbers who thereby extended their training possibilities, some by tough walkers with no climbing aspirations. During the 1920s there was a Bog-Trotters Club which carried out many tough long-distance walks across moors and hills; many expeditions of this type were made in subsequent years by all sorts of people. These took the form of long day walks, such as Marsden to Edale, which could be done between the first train out in the morning and the last one home at night, or week-end walks involving the crossing of some of the moors in the dark in trips of, say, 50 to 75 miles taking 20 to 30 hours. Typical of these are Colne to Rowsley down the eastern gritstone escarpment or Colne to Leek down the western. Another is the Four Inns Walk from the site of the former 'Isle of Skye Inn', near Marsden, to 'Flouch Inn', near Penistone, over Bleaklow to 'Snake Inn', then over Kinder to Hayfield and down the western moors to the 'Cat and Fiddle' on the Buxton–Macclesfield Road. This last, the second highest in England, is named, incidentally, after a knight, Caton le Fidele, and has no connection with the nursery rhyme. Looking round for a suitable long walk to commemorate their fiftieth anniversary, the Rucksack Club of Manchester hit on the idea of linking the two highest inns in England—'Tan Hill' in North Yorkshire and the 'Cat and Fiddle'. This marathon of 120 miles, 20,000 feet of ascent, 50 hours and two nights out, was done at Whitsun, 1952, by three members and repeated the following year by three others. The organization required makes this sort of trip a group activity, but very long walks like these provide perhaps the only opportunity for extended effort in English mountains, and thus real training for protracted expeditions in the great ranges of the world.

Between the Peak and the Welsh border are the plains of Cheshire, broken only by the Peckforton Hills (729 feet). The ruins of Beeston Castle stand on top of a steep crag where climbing has been done; this is yet another of the loads of stones dropped around the country by the Devil in his travels. Farther north, Helsby and Frodsham Hills, the former with a fine climbers' crag, look down on to the industrial north of the county.

From the Peak District the Pennines run northwards forming the 'Backbone of England' or as Camden puts it: 'Like the Apennine in Italy, with a continued ridge rising more with continued tops and cliffs one after another ever as far as Scotland.' Along the 250 miles between Edale in Derbyshire and Kirk Yetholm just over the Scottish border the Pennine Way works its way by hill and ridge through the very best of the scenery.

Between the northern edge of the Peak and the line of the Aire and the lower Ribble is an area of high, lonely moorland dissected by deep valleys which are highly industrialized. Camden called all this Blackstone Edge, but this is in fact a ridge crowned with gritstone outcrops above Littleborough on the Rochdale–Halifax road. There is a well-preserved 'Roman' road here but archaeologists differ as to its exact origin. An early traveller to pass this way was Celia Fiennes, who noticed in 1698, as we still do today, how the moors 'stagnate the aire and hold miste and raines almost perpetually'. Later Defoe crossed in a snow-storm, detecting here with his customary imagination 'the Andes of England' (he found the Breconshire mountains like the Andes also!). To the south are Standedge and the Saddleworth Moors, black peat and

12 Snowdon from Cwm D

tussocky grass, crossed in various places by high roads from Lancashire to Yorkshire. All the road summits are above 1,000 feet and these are the places where winter snows quickly block the flow of industrial traffic from side to side of the range. Holme Moss carries a lofty television mast. Beyond Blackstone Edge the moors expand northwards. On Heptonstall Moor at Widdop is a gritstone crag which was called Mystery Buttress because its discoverers did not immediately publicize their find and for a long time no one knew exactly where it was. The moorland around Haworth close to Keighley is the Brontë country.

The Forest of Rossendale is a westward extension of the high country into Lancashire—moors again of grass, heather and peat, with the industrial towns of Bolton, Rochdale, Blackburn and Burnley at the four corners, yet for all that wild and comparatively lonely. Above Burnley to the north 'lying like a leviathan basking in the sunshine' looms the great mass of Pendle Hill. This seven-mile ridge, reaching 1,831 feet, dominates the landscape of north Lancashire. The summit provides contrasting views—on the one hand towards industry, on the other across the pastoral valley of the Ribble to the clean grey limestone mountains of Craven and to Bowland Forest, which at Ward's Hill overtops it by only five feet. Three times in the last 300 years so-called 'water-brasts', sometimes attributed to witchcraft, flowed down Pendle side and devastated the surroundings. Porous gritstone here rests on sloping beds of impervious shale; after exceptional rainfall the large volume of water held up inside the hill washes away some of the shale, which flows down admixed with water and peat.

North of the Aire and west of the Wharfe is the district of Craven, of which Camden writes: ' . . . perchance of the British word Crage, that is a Stone. For the whole tract there is rough all over, and unpleasant to see to; with craggie stones, hanging rockes, and rugged waies.' The 'craggie stones and hanging rockes' are mostly of light coloured mountain limestone, which because of pronounced faulting forms steep crags above ground and deep caves below.

The verticals and overhangs of Malham Cove, Gordale Scar, Kilnsey Crag and the rest are outstandingly impressive as also are the awesome shafts of the potholes. Here and there the hills have a cap of gritstone, notably the famous 'three peaks' of Ingleborough, Whernside and Penyghent, which cluster round the head of Ribblesdale. The round of these is another pleasant walk, turned into a marathon in recent years by cross-country runners, who can cover it in about 4½ hours. (The latest 'record' is 3 hours 17 minutes.) Ingleborough (2,373 feet) is a massive flat-topped mountain, measuring five miles round the 2,000-foot contour. Early remains have been found on the summit which was later used as a military post and a beacon by the Romans. West (1780), who believed the height to be 3,987 feet, tells us that the remains of a beacon were still visible then and that horse races were held at one time on the top. Wilkinson, who climbed the hill some 40 years later, found real difficulties:

> . . . as a child learning to walk and afraid of falling, creeps on his hands and knees, thus, to gratify my ambition, I crawled among the rocks fallen from the summit of the mountain. I durst not look behind me, lest my head should become giddy; so with alternate glimpses to what was above me, I looked right down to earth; consequently, my prospect extended but a few yards . . . .

But he made it. Subsequent history tells of the construction of a tower of refuge on the summit, demolished quickly in riots which attended the opening ceremony, and of a projected mountain railway from Ingleton, fortunately never more than an idea. For many years now an annual race has been run from Ingleton to the summit and back; this is regularly done in less than an hour. Another striking feature of lime-stone country, well seen on Ingleborough, is the so-called limestone pavement; where, over wide plateau areas, bare rock is exposed at the surface and trenched by irregular chasms, known as clints or grikes, coinciding with the joint planes.

There are wonderful caves in the limestone plinth of the mountain, including Gaping Gill, Britain's most famous pothole, first descended by the French speleologist, E. A. Martel, in 1895. The main chamber is 500 feet by 90 feet by 110 feet high and its floor is 330 feet below the surface of the moor. The shaft, only 30 feet by 15 feet at the surface, can be descended by rope ladder, as Martel did, but periodically a donkey engine and a wire hawser enable cavers to go down by bosun's chair—a startling and extremely interesting experience. Other famous caves of Craven include Alum Pot (a cleft 130 feet long and 290 feet deep—'like the spathe, black instead of white, of an enormous arum lily'), Lost John's (2 miles long and 500 feet deep), Nick Pot (with an underground ladder pitch of 260 feet) and the show caves of Ingleborough and White Scar. There are dozens more and every year diligent exploration produces fresh discoveries and extensions.

Whernside (2,419 feet), a long whale-back, is a few miles north of Ingleborough; Penyghent (2,273 feet), 'the crouching lion with scarred flanks', a few miles east beyond the Ribble.

Wharfedale, which forms the eastern boundary of Craven, is dominated by the great overhangs of Kilnsey Crag, scene of some very hard mechanized climbing in recent years. There have been occasions when spectators watching climbers in action have caused traffic blocks on the road below and there has even been a threat by authorities to put the crag out of bounds. East again, Nidderdale is 'water supply landscape' and there are several reservoirs; nearby are the caves of Goyden Pot and Manchester Hole and gritstone crags at Guisecliff and Brimham. The grotesque scenery of the latter, including fantasies such as Idol Rock (a 200-ton boulder on a 12-inch-diameter stalk), has attracted the attention of passing travellers for centuries past. North of these two valleys there are no longer any notable crags or caves and the rest of the Pennines is purely walkers' country.

The Yorkshire Dales, lying to the north and east of Wharfedale, comprise the valleys of the Nidd, the Ure (Wensleydale) and the Swale, all east-flowing feeders of the Yorkshire Ouse. The natural boundary on the north side is the Stainmore Gap, which joins the valley of the Eden on the west with that of the Greta and the Tees on the east. This was a route used by Bronze Age traders, later defended by a large Roman camp; nowadays it carries the main road from Scotch Corner to Penrith, crossing a summit of 1,436 feet between Bowes, site of Dickens's Dotheboys Hall, and Brough. A huge area of the Dales, plus a large part of Craven, forms the Yorkshire Dales National Park with an area of about 700 square miles.

It is the valleys that dominate; in the words of Geoffrey Young— 'the skyline is little regarded, and the hills are but supports, between which the folds and hollows of the dales are suspended in noble curves of ever changing tension'. However, the hills still serve as barriers to communication. Between Wharfedale and Nidderdale is Great Whernside (2,310 feet), which though 'Great' by name is less so in height than the Whernside of the Three Peaks. The road from Wharfedale to Bishopsdale and Wensleydale reaches 1,376 feet below Buckden Pike and that from Langstrothdale to Wensleydale over Fleet Moss 1,832 feet. The Buttertubs Pass (1,726 feet), named after a series of deep holes in the limestone near its summit, crosses from Wensleydale to Swaledale between Great Shunner Fell (2,340 feet), the highest hill hereabouts, and Lovely Seat. Farther north still on the road from Arkengarthdale over to Stainmore is 'Tan Hill Inn' (1,732 feet), the highest in England.

The hills of the Pennines north of Stainmore, between there and the South Tyne, are shared between North Riding, Westmorland, Cumberland and Durham. Here is Mickle Fell (2,591 feet) the highest point in Yorkshire, soon, it is said, to be set aside as a Nature Reserve and closed to the public. A few miles farther north, actually in Cumberland, is Cross Fell (2,930 feet), the highest point of the range and of England outside the Lake District. This was climbed in 1747 by George Smith, a geographer, who sent an account to the *Gentleman's Magazine*: 'a mountain that is generally ten months bury'd in snow, and eleven in clouds, cannot fail of exciting the attraction and curiosity of a traveller'. They set out from Alston and were soon 'environ'd with large and extended morasses, rocks and mountains that exhibited a very frightful appearance', on past the lead mines at Bulmanscleugh, and then:

> We had now ascended gradually about 3 miles, thro' very broken morassy wastes, when the mountain began to rise in three very formidable ascents, very steep, in the manner of Mount Lebanon, pil'd one above another, with large and extensive plains to each of them, and loose shivery stones on brows, very troublesome to the horses which we were now obliged sometimes to quit. This continued for near 2 miles more, when we got on the edge of the highest, which forms a capacious plain of several hundred acres, if you reckon from the East ascent; but of such a barren soil, that there was not so much as a single leaf of grass, herb or plant to be found in so large a plain, exclusive of a few of those rings attributed to fairies . . . This immense plain has no verdure, therefore, but a venerably grey aspect from the moss or down, and even this can hardly draw a subsistence to support itself; so inconceivably barren is this distinguished eminence.

He was tremendously impressed by the view and surprised not to find 'any the least relicks of snow'.

For hundreds of years Cross Fell has been noted for the Helm Wind which, when the prevailing wind is north-easterly, blows with great violence down the treeless south-western slopes. A wall of cloud, the Helm, appears above the summit at this time, while another cloud line called the Bar can be seen five miles or so south-west. Below the latter there is little or no wind. The whole process is a result of the configuration of the ground, the hill behaving in the air stream much as a submerged weir does in the bed of a river. More than 100 years ago Wilkinson noted this singular phenomenon as follows:

> An assemblage of pale clouds extends on the summit of the mountain; and, when all is calm on the plains, a roaring like the sea is heard to a considerable distance. I was once involved in the Helm Wind—if I advanced, it was with my head inclined to the ground, and at a slow pace; if I retreated and leaned against it with all my might, I could hardly keep erect; if I did not resist it, I was blown over. A wind from the east rushed down the mountain with incredible fury; it broke the boughs from the trees, and tore the thatch from cottages at Mellerby and Gamelsby. But when I had left this elemental tumult about two miles, all was perfectly calm, and a little further a gentle breeze sprung up from the west, while behind me the Helm Wind continued raging with unabated fury.

Cross Fell, Mickle Fell and the intervening hills form the scarp edge of a great block of peaty moorland and bleak pasture, which slopes down gradually eastward to the plains of the Durham coalfield. Lead and zinc were mined here in mediaeval times, if not earlier. The block is dissected by the Rivers Tees, Wear, Derwent and South Tyne. Centrally sited is Alston, which at an altitude of 900 feet is reputed to be the highest market town in England. A few miles to the east the road over to Weardale (B6293) is the highest classified road in England, crossing a summit of no less than 2,056 feet. There is little millstone grit now and, though the rocks are still Carboniferous, the pure limestone which characterizes this period farther south is replaced by alternating beds of sandstone, limestone and clays. Intruded among them and outcropping all over the area is a sheet of igneous rock called the Whin Sill. This has resisted erosion better than the other rocks and forms distinctive physical features—the waterfall of High Force in Teesdale, the crags at High Cup Nick, the rocky edge followed by the

Roman Wall and seacliffs at Cullernose, Dunstanburgh and the Farne Islands.

The Roman Wall, 73½ miles long, built after Hadrian's visit to Britain about A.D. 121, crossed the country from Wallsend on the Tyne to Bowness on Solway Firth. One of the best preserved sections is near the fort of Housesteads. Close by at Crag Lough, where the Wall runs impregnably along the edge of the Whin Sill, modern climbers now scale the rocks beneath. From this point the Northumberland National Park stretches north and east almost to the Scottish border, except where, round the headwaters of the North Tyne, it is National Forest Park instead. This is Kielder Forest, which with 46,000 acres of plantations is the largest in Britain; it is part of the 200 square miles of the Border Forest Park, which continues far into Roxburghshire. The carboniferous sandstone, known as Fell Sandstone, outcropping across Northumberland to the sea at Berwick, reaches 1,447 feet at Tosson Hill near Rothbury. There are climbers' crags on Simonside nearby and also at Great Wanney by Sweethope Lough, both of which were climbed on by local enthusiasts over 50 years ago.

Between these Carboniferous rocks and the Scottish border are lavas and igneous rocks forming the Cheviot. This is a vast stretch of whale-back hills, on which it is said a 25-mile route can be made without crossing even a cart-track, while in the whole distance between Crag Lough and Yeavering Bell near Wooler there is but one main road and one secondary road. The vegetation here is different from that of the Pennines farther south, the rough fell grass and heather replaced by smoother, finer grass with scattered plantations of trees. In the words of one modern writer: 'it is a scenery of great wind-swept, rain-washed, sun-splashed, cloud-dappled panoramas'.

The Cheviot itself, at 2,676 feet the highest point of the county, gives an easy climb to a summit which, being both extensive and almost flat, is all peat bog. There are a few rock climbs around, at Henhole and Bizzle for example, and ski-ing is almost always available on the wide unbroken slopes in the winter months. Defoe reached the summit in 1726 going nearly all the way on horseback. At length they feared to go farther with the beasts and alighting, continued on foot:

> We were the more uneasy about mounting higher, because we all had a
> Notion, that when we came to the Top, we should be just as upon a

Pinnacle, that the Hill narrowed to a Point, and we should have only Room enough to stand, with a Precipice every way round us; and with these Apprehensions, we all sat down upon the Ground, and said we would go no farther.

Their guide made light of their fears, assuring them that there was room on top to run a race if they so desired; they pressed on, therefore, and were up half an hour later:

I must acknowledge I was agreeably surprised, when coming to the Top of the Hill, I saw before me a smooth, and with respect to what we expected a most pleasant Plain, of at least half a Mile in Diameter; and in the Middle of it a large Pond, or little Lake of Water, and the Ground seeming to descend every way from the Edges of the Summit to the Pond, took off the little Terror of the first Prospect.

He descended by the same route, finding as many of us still do, that 'it is much more troublesome, and also tiresome to come down than to go up'.

These are the last few miles of the Pennine Way, which terminates down below at Kirk Yetholm. From this last great hill on the Way the traveller looks out across the first of the hills of Scotland and these stretch northwards 'a countless herd of hills, tossing their shining muzzles in the sun' almost without interruption to Cape Wrath and John o' Groats.

Wedged, as we have already noted, between the heavily populated industrial areas of Lancashire and Yorkshire, the southern portion of the Pennines plays a big part in the lives of many people who enjoy the extreme contrast between this countryside and the drabness, the smoke and the bustle of their towns. As in the adjacent Peak, they find three activities predominating—hill walking, caving and rock climbing; these have a certain amount of overlap, yet are ultimately widely divergent.

Rock climbing was first carried out on various outcrops of gritstone, such as Laddow Rocks near Greenfield and Almscliff between Leeds and Harrogate, which were in use before the turn of the century. Later, as the sport developed, more out-of-the-way crags were opened up, for example in the hills between Skipton and Grassington, in Nidderdale and so on. Brimham Rocks in Nidderdale had in fact been noted by Haskett Smith:

. . . Nowhere are the grotesque forms which millstone grit delights to assume more remarkable. Some resemble the sandstone forms common about Tunbridge Wells, and many might very well stand for Dartmoor Tors; but others at first sight seem so evidently and unmistakably to suggest human handiwork that one can feel no surprise at the common notion that they were fashioned by the ingenuity of the Druids.

Even so, they were not seriously climbed upon until about 1950. Gritstone continues to enjoy an established and deserved popularity.

The great limestone crags on the other hand were not climbed upon until after the Second World War, when they emerged rather suddenly as training grounds for the new sport of artificial, or mechanized, climbing. This involves the provision of the holds by hammering pitons into existing cracks or by fitting expansion bolts into holes specially drilled in the rock. Rope loops or short rope ladders (*étriers*) attached to the spikes or bolts by snap rings (*karabiners*) are additionally used as footholds in overhanging places. The leader is safeguarded by running his rope through a snap ring attached to a bolt or piton above his head and his companions can hold him in position with the aid of this rope while he concentrates on the next move on the climb. In practice it is somewhat more complicated, but the above gives some idea of the salient features. It will be appreciated that this sort of work, all done on vertical or overhanging faces, is very exacting and is only for the few. The first artificial climbing in Yorkshire was done in 1956, when routes were made on Gordale Scar and Kilnsey Crag, each requiring about 30 pitons. The first ascent of Malham Cove in 1958 by T. Peck and the Biven brothers took 12 pitons, 85 ring screws, 24 battered chisels and 58 hours and was graded V.S. and A4. Here is a small part of T. Peck's story:

. . . From my topmost ring screw on the wall right underneath the overhang, I was able, by leaning well out, to get a small peg in a doubtful looking crack low down on the face of the overhang. In transferring oneself to this peg, one goes for an agonising swing into space 300 feet directly above ground. My only hope at the time was that the peg would hold. It held, and the scenery took on a decidedly more pleasant aspect . . . One more doubtful peg, another ring screw and two very good pegs, and I was at the top.

The peg under the overhang came out when the second man trusted his weight to it; held by the leader above he swung out and hung clear in

14 *Kilnsey Crag, Wharfe*

space. Now the only possible method of regaining contact with the rock was to climb the rope and this he did, continuing without further mishap to join the leader at the top.

Extensive developments are taking place everywhere and these methods are now firmly a part of the British climbing scene.

Yorkshire owes its pre-eminence in the world of caving to the great thickness of the limestone strata (around 500 feet) and the heavy local faulting. Originally the limestone was formed from the consolidated remains of marine life laid down in beds on the floor of some ancient sea. Later the now-solid rocks were uplifted mightily and, in the process, tilted and cracked through the mass. It happens that limestone is dissolved slowly by surface water which is for any reason slightly acidic. Rain water, therefore, sinking into the system of vertical cracks (joints) and horizontal cracks (bedding planes) gradually enlarges the path through which it flows. The process is accelerated as the streams get big enough to carry stones which can abrade the side walls and bed. Systems of caves are thus formed with tunnels, vertical shafts (called potholes) and wide low passages (bedding planes). If a stream wearing away its bed breaks eventually into another joint, the whole of the water is deflected into a new system leaving the original tunnels dry and streamless; the whole hill-side becomes honeycombed with cavities. Caves high on the hill, where the surface water disappears into the rock, are called caves of engulfment. Several hundred feet lower the cave system becomes waterlogged and the caver can only in rare instances penetrate further. The water can and does, however, and emerges from the rock once again where it meets lower impervious strata at another cave, called this time a rising or a cave of debouchure. Thus the waters which disappear at Gaping Gill reappear at Ingleborough Cave, and so on. The sport of caving poses some interesting problems of penetrating from an engulfment to a rising, or reversely, and most of these are still far from solution.

That monumental volume *British Caving* sums it up as follows: 'Caving is the most absolute of sports. It matches the thrills of exploring the unknown and defying physical obstacles with the intellectual challenge to explain how the unfamiliar shapes and beauties of underground scenery have evolved.' This is substantially true—certainly caves provide the only opportunity for original exploration available

ledgehope Hill from
heviot

97

to most of us in a country so thickly populated. The big drawback is that it all takes place in the dark away from the sunshine. Down there all sensations are dulled so that, when the caver returns to the surface, he is vividly aware of the marvellous smell of fresh air and of vegetation and flowers. Perhaps the best answer is to cave by night and to sunbathe by day.

Of the three sports, walking provides the greatest range of experience and touches on the lives of the most people. The motorist can travel further in a shorter time, but for him the hills are nothing but a background; only the walker can penetrate almost everywhere and see almost everything. The extra experiences he would have as a climber or a caver could not completely compensate him for what he would miss by concentrating solely on districts of crag and cavern. On the other hand the physical endeavour, the mastery of technique and the heightened sensations of climbing and caving enrich the hill-lover's experience, so that the best method must be, if at all possible, to indulge in all of them.

The outstanding walk here, the Pennine Way, is comparable in principle, though not in magnitude, with the great mountain trails of North America. Essentially it is a high-level route between Kinder Scout in Derbyshire and the Cheviot in Northumberland crossing in between such Pennine tops as Bleaklow, Black Hill, Standedge, Blackstone Edge, Stoodley Pike, Fountains Fell, Penyghent, Dodd Fell, Great Shunner Fell and Cross Fell. It is partly rough paths and trackways with occasional signposts, while way-marking on high ground is done by cairns or stakes. Some of the more remote parts are for experienced hill walkers only, and they will need a compass and an adequate map for comfort and safety. It is necessary to turn aside in places to find overnight accommodation, though in fine weather sleeping out would everywhere be practical. Though the idea of the Way was first mooted in 1935 and the whole length had been surveyed before the war, it was not until 1951 that the scheme received government approval under the National Parks and Access to the Countryside Act, 1949. Even then the 'rights-of-way' arrangements were not completed for the whole distance until 1965.

FIVE

Lake District
National Park

Between the Pennines and the western sea, and divided between the counties of Cumberland, Westmorland and Lancashire, lies the Lake District, 900 square miles of which were designated a National Park in May, 1951. On 70 of these square miles the average annual rainfall exceeds 100 inches! Here are England's highest, wildest and most attractive mountains. Camden, who shows no signs of the dread which afflicted later travellers, certainly found them that way:

> Although it be somewhat with the coldest, as lying farre North, and seemeth by reason of hilles, yet for the variety thereof it smileth upon the beholders, and giveth contentment to as many as travaile it. For, after the rockes bunching out, the mountains standing thick together, rich of mettal mines, and betweene them great meeres stored with all kinds of wild fowls, you come to pretty hills for good pasturage and well replenished with flocks of sheep, beneath which again you meet with goodly plaines spreading out a great way, yielding corne sufficiently.

A century and a half later Defoe was impressed in a quite different way, describing Westmorland as 'a county eminent only for being the wildest, most barren and frightful of any that I have passed over in England or even in Wales itself; the west side, which borders on Cumberland, is indeed bounded by a chain of almost unpassable mountains'. There seems some doubt, however, whether Defoe really went there, but rather gave his public from a distance what he felt they wanted.

The first opening up of the Lake District took place during the last quarter of the eighteenth century when several worthy travellers toured around and later published accounts of their journeys. They included Thomas Pennant (1769), whom we have met in Wales, now passing through on his way to Scotland, Thomas Gray (1769), the poet of the *Elegy*, William Gilpin (1772), a Hampshire clergyman, and William Hutchinson (1773–74), attorney from Durham. The first guidebook was produced by Father Thomas West in 1778 and this ran to many editions in the next few decades. He listed 'stations' from which the best views could be seen; he advocated standing with back to the scenery and viewing it in a plano-convex landscape mirror—'where objects are great and near it removes them to a due distance, and shows them in the soft colours of nature, and in the most regular perspective the eye can perceive or science demonstrate'; he recommended a telescope—'for viewing the fronts and summits of inaccessible rocks, and the distant country from the tops of the high mountains Skiddaw and Helvellyn'.

For all of these the mountains were not much more than a background to the scenery of the valleys. The first mountain walker, of what we may perhaps call the modern type, was Captain Joseph Budworth, one-armed ex-soldier, who came in the 1790s. He not only ascended Skiddaw and Helvellyn, which were occasionally done at the time, but also Fairfield, Dollywaggon Pike, Coniston Old Man, Helm Crag, and so on. He enjoyed it all tremendously—for example, trundling boulders down the slopes of Helvellyn. 'Many have been delighted', he says, 'in tumbling boulders down young hills; they may therefore imagine a large stone bounding off with a great bow, then darting from side to side of indented ragged chasms, until it jumped upon a heap of stones, or hopped distantly into the valley.' In 1797 he made what was probably the first tourist ascent of the Langdale Pikes. At the valley farmhouse from which he started they told him that 'they never remembered foine folk aiming at et afore'; higher up Budworth and his young guide found 'many rough rocks to scramble up, and in a deep recess, impenetrable to the sun, a large quantity of snow that I should suppose never completely dissolves. We had again to haul ourselves by rocks to bring us to the crown of Langdale Pike, which is about twenty yards in circumference, with in the centre a small natural stone seat.' And Budworth's motive for climbing, as told to his guide—'Curiosity'.

William Wordsworth, who was born in Cockermouth in 1770, came back to live in the Lake District in 1799 and stayed till his death in 1850. He wrote a guidebook, which was reprinted several times, including in later editions an account of his ascent of Scafell Pike. Southey lived in the district for many years; Coleridge and de Quincey came for a time—a talented gathering. Coleridge made a very early ascent of Scafell and Scafell Pike in 1802.

The area became more and more popular and guidebooks proliferated

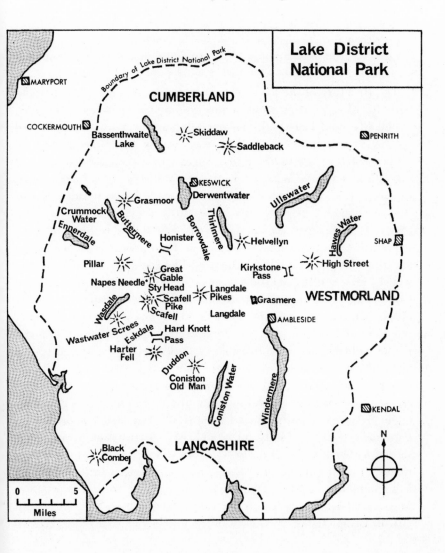

—mostly, however, very cautious in their descriptions of even the simplest mountain ascents and crossings. More than 40 years after Coleridge, Otley's *Guide* could still write of the highest mountain:

> Scawfell Pikes may be ascended on foot from any of the adjacent vales, but most conveniently from Borrowdale; yet the distance from a place of entertainment, the ruggedness of the ground, the danger of being caught in a cloud—to which, from its situation, it is more subject than its neighbours—altogether conspire against its being visited by any other than by hardy pedestrians: and strangers should so calculate their time, that night may not overtake them in such places; to be enveloped in a cloud is of itself disagreeable, cloud and night together would be dreadful.

The structure of the Lake District is simple. A huge dome of rocks with its highest point along a line joining the present mountains, Scafell Pike and Helvellyn, and once drained by a series of outward flowing rivers, has been eroded away leaving the radial pattern of valleys which we see today. Wordsworth wrote the classic account of the hills and valleys in his *Description of the Scenery of the Lakes* (1810), though it is said that the ideas expressed were by no means original. 'Let us suppose', he said, 'our station to be a cloud hanging midway between Great Gavel (Great Gable) and Scafell . . . we shall then see stretched at our feet a number of valleys, not fewer than eight, diverging from the point on which we stand, like spokes from the nave of a wheel.' First comes Langdale leading on to Windermere, then Coniston ('not as the other valleys do to the nave of the wheel, and therefore it may be not inaptly represented as a broken spoke sticking in the rim'), the vale of Duddon, the vale of Esk, the deep valley of Wasdale ('with its little chapel and half a dozen neat dwellings scattered upon a plain of meadow and corn ground, intersected with stone walls apparently innumerable, like a large piece of lawless patchwork, or an array of mathematical figures, such as in the ancient schools of geometry might have been sportively and fantastically traced out upon sand'), Ennerdale, the vale of Buttermere and lastly Borrowdale, of which the vale of Keswick is a continuation. 'From this it would seem', he continues, 'that the image of a wheel, this far exact, is little more than half complete . . . take a flight therefore of not more than four or five miles eastward to a point on the ridge of Helvellyn.' The circle can now be completed by Wythburn and St John's Vale, Ullswater, Haweswater and lastly by the vales of Grasmere, Rydal and Ambleside. Here then the valleys and lakes dominate the scenery and we think in terms of the mountains accessible from each of the valleys rather than of mountain groups as we did in North Wales. The layout of the hills has helped considerably to retain the wildness of the central core; thus today there are motor roads across Honister Pass from Buttermere to Borrowdale, Newlands Pass from Buttermere to Newlands, Whinlatter Pass from Buttermere to Keswick, Wrynose from Little Langdale to Duddon and Hard Knott from Duddon to Eskdale, but all other crossings from valley to valley can only be made by foot-track. Proposals for 'opening up' some of these with motor roads have been made from time to time, notably for Sty Head just after World War I, but so far always unsuccessfully.

There are three principal rock series; north and west of Derwentwater are the Skiddaw Slates, forming shapely smooth-sided mountains of which Skiddaw is the highest. Centrally lie the volcanic Borrowdale Slates, where we find the most rugged and the highest mountains as well as all the climbers' crags, while in the south-east corner of the region around Windermere and Coniston Water the Bannisdale Slates outcrop in lower wooded hills seldom reaching 1,000 feet. Fourteen of the lakes exceed a mile in length. Some of the smaller ones lie in basins hollowed out by glacier action, but most of the valley lakes have resulted from the damming of the valleys by glacial drift. Wastwater, the deepest, is 280 feet. The various valleys, some with their lakes, others without, and the steep-sided mountains grouped around, have a marked individuality and there are very few places that can be called dull or featureless.

Wasdale, with Scafell, Scafell Pike, Great Gable, Kirkfell and Yewbarrow grouped round its head is the centre of the highest and wildest mountains. Haskett Smith, before his first visit, picked it out from the Ordnance Survey Map as 'a sombre region thronged with portentous shadows', the copious hachuring indicating precipitous slopes on every hand. But it had a reputation before that. In the 1820s this was indeed a remote valley, as the author of *Pleasure Tours* told his readers—'the lake is of very difficult access, except on the side of Egremont, and few travellers care to encounter the dangers of the Alpine ways that lead to it'. On the other hand T. Wilkinson in the same period expressed sentiments that we can still echo—'Though attended with difficulty, who would regret that once in his life he had come down Great Gable to explore the wonders of Wast Water?' (who, indeed!) 'The mountains of Wast Water', he continued, 'are naked to their bases; their sides and their summits are uniform; their summits shoot up into lofty points, and end in the form of pyramids. We have heard of the Pyramids of Egypt, built by the hand of man; but these are the Pyramids of the world, built by the Architect of the Universe.'

Scafell Pike (3,210 feet), the highest point of Cumberland and of England, is a straightforward climb either from Wasdale up Brown Tongue or from the top of Esk Hause over Broad Crag. The summit was given to the National Trust many years ago as a Memorial to the men of the Lake District who fell in World War I. Scafell (3,162 feet), recently described as a 'remarkable combination of a slightly commonplace hump and the most savage barrier of naked rock and scree in England', faces the Pike across the col of Mickledore. From here the latter is easily accessible, but Scafell throws down great crags on either side of the col and these join together across it in a low wall, which bars access to pedestrians. An easy, but slightly exposed, rock climb must be done to pass from one mountain to the other, or else a long detour made round the crags on either hand into Eskdale or Wasdale. The best known of these short rock routes is Broad Stand, believed to have been descended by the poet Coleridge in 1802 and climbed around 1820 by two local dalesmen. It is a tricky passage for the inexperienced, particularly if there is ice about.

The col at the head of the main valley above Wasdale is called Sty Head and a well-marked track runs this way, past Sprinkling Tarn where the average annual rainfall exceeds 150 inches, down to Seathwaite in Borrowdale, the wettest inhabited place in England. Gray was inexplicably reticent about the Sty Head path, writing of it: 'All further access is here barred to prying mortals; only there is a little path winding over the fells, and for some weeks in the year passable to dalesmen', even though he must have known where it went. In any case it was surveyed on a scale of one inch to one mile in the following year. From Sty Head summit another track branches southeastwards to Esk Hause (2,490 ft.), continuing past Angle Tarn and down Rossett Gill to Langdale. This is an important pedestrian route—

the distance is a mere eight miles, but for the motorist these valleys are some 40 miles apart round the outskirts of the hills.

The square pyramid of Great Gable (2,949 feet), once perhaps Great Gavel, rises immediately above Wasdale Head. During the 1920s the summits of this and eleven other of the surrounding mountains were purchased by the Fell and Rock Climbing Club and presented to the National Trust as a War Memorial. All four ridges give straight-forward ascents to the top, in between are steeper slopes with climbers' crags on the south called the Napes, and on the north above Ennerdale. Haskett Smith was the first to draw attention to the curious ruin of a man-made shelter half-way up the latter crag. 'This was', he wrote, 'a ruined hut thickly overgrown with moss, and showing no trace of any wood having been employed in its construction. The spot had evidently been chosen primarily with a view to concealment, and the result of enquiries kindly made since then by one of my friends has been to elicit proof of certain traditions still lingering among the older inhabitants of these dales concerning a noted distiller of illicit spirits, who flourished and defied the law among these wild retreats.' There may be some connection between this and an ancient trackway, known as Moses' Sledgate, which has been traced from near Seatoller at the back of Brandreth, round the head of Ennerdale below the crags on Gable, over Beck Head, and down the south-west ridge of Gable into Wasdale. Moses may well have used this route in the heydey of smuggling, but it is probable that the way itself goes back even further into history.

From Wasdale we ascend the side valley of Mosedale and cross the pass of Black Sail into Ennerdale. This is an easy route, yet less than 100 years ago the usually reliable Black's *Guide* was describing it in these generous terms: 'The hardy pedestrian with very minute instructions might succeed in finding his way over the mountains, yet everyone who has crossed them will beware of the danger of the attempt and of the occasional fatal consequences attending a diversion from the proper path.' Haskett Smith comments—'the enterprising traveller who only breaks his neck two or three times in the course of the journey will be of good cheer.'

Ennerdale is the only one of the major valleys without a road to its head, and indeed it benefits considerably from this good fortune,

retaining perhaps some hint of those attributes which caused Whellan
to write in 1860—'Ennerdale Lake . . . is so wild in the character of
its shores and in its position among the mountains as to have caused
more terrors and disasters to strangers than any other spot in the
district.'

The valley, much afforested in the upper part in the years between
the Wars, is dominated by the great Pillar Rock, which rises from the
slopes of Pillar Mountain:

> You see yon precipice, it wears the shape
> Of a vast building made of many crags;
> And in the midst is one particular rock
> That rises like a column from the vale,
> Whence by our shepherds it is called the Pillar (Wordsworth).

The summit (the Promised Land) is cut off from the main fellside
(Pisgah) by a gap 50 feet deep (Jordan Gap). There is no pedestrian
route, though the simplest ways are extremely easy rock climbs. The
first ascent was made by John Atkinson, a local cooper, in 1826.

We climb out of Ennerdale over the Red Pike Group by the pass
of Scarth Gap, descending on the other side to Buttermere with its
three lakes backed by the vast bulk of Grassmoor. Here, too, are the
quaintly named peaks of Haystacks (possibly from the Norse word
'stack', possibly on account of its shape) and Robinson. The motorist
is well catered for with three passes over to Borrowdale and Keswick
and though these are steep and narrow, they are considerably used.

Borrowdale is perhaps the finest of the Lakeland valleys. Leland says
of it—'Divers springes cummeth owt of Borodale, and so make a great
Lowgh that we cawle a Poole'. The pool is of course Derwentwater
and beyond that lies another great lake, Bassenthwaite. Between them
is Keswick, the most important town of the Lake District, though we
no longer describe it in the words of two centuries ago:

> . . . Rocks and cliffs of stupendous height hanging broken over the lake
> in horrible grandeur, some of them a thousand feet high, the woods climb-
> ing up their steep and shaggy sides, where mortal foot never yet approached.
> On these dreadful heights the eagles build their nests . . . while on all sides of
> this immense amphitheatre the lofty mountains rise around, piercing the
> clouds in shapes as spiry and fantastic as the very rocks of Dovedale . . .

The full perfection of Keswick consists of three circumstances, beauty, horror and immensity united.

The most important of the lofty mountains is Skiddaw (3,058 feet), a huge rounded bulk of a mountain, 'the red glare' on which, rousing the burghers of Carlisle at Armada time, formed the last link in the chain of warning fires which had spread through the length of England. Camden quotes Skiddaw as one of the highest points in England, later Defoe reported similarly. Early travellers seem to have been impressed by the thinness of the air—'respiration seemed to be performed with a kind of oppression'—we all know the feeling. Nowadays it is a very easy climb, even a motor car has been to the top; in the words of a local bard:

> Laal brag it is for any man
> To clim oop Skidder side;
> Auld wives and bairns on Jackasses
> To tippy twop ma ride.

North-east of Skiddaw above the Penrith Road is Saddleback (or Blencathra) another mountain so extensive that it has been said that 'if you could hollow out Blencathra you would have a dish cover that would fit over London'. Though this too is a very easy mountain it inspired early travellers no less—'the views from the summit are exceedingly extensive, but those immediately under the eye on the mountain itself so tremendous and appalling that few persons have sufficient resolution to experience the emotions which those awful scenes inspire'. There is an account of an ascent made in 1798:

> When we had ascended about a mile, one of the party, on looking round, was so astonished with the different appearance of objects in the valley so far beneath us that he declined proceeding. We had not gone much further till the other companion (of the relator) was suddenly taken ill and wished to loose blood and return.

John Peel, that most famous of huntsmen, was born near Caldbeck north of Saddleback in the 1770s. His song, known nowadays by every school-child, has become traditional, surprisingly, in little more than a century. Local foxhunting has continued to be popular; the huntsmen follow the hounds on foot over crag and rocky hillside, keeping up as they may; the hounds run sometimes for remarkable distances, 50 miles or more has been known, picking up new followers as they go. No doubt all but the fox enjoy this immensely, but even if he is regarded as vermin, is this necessarily the best way of exterminating him?

The hills between Borrowdale and the next valley of Wythburn and St John lack distinction, but beyond the partially artificial lake of Thirlmere—water supply for Manchester—rises the long ridge of Helvellyn (3,118 feet), third highest and most climbed mountain of the Lake District. It has been ascended on pony-back; bicycles and motor-cycles have been taken to the summit, and even in 1926 an aeroplane. The author of *Pleasure Tours* (1822) found little to recommend on the west side: 'Of all the rude and terrific scenery yet passed, none equals this in desolation and dreariness. The whole is one immensity of barrenness. The mountains are universally overspread with crags and stones, which are sometimes scattered carelessly over their surfaces, and sometimes appear shivering in cascades of crumbling fragments down their sides.' To the east, however, the rock scenery is very fine. Red Tarn, 750 feet below the summit, is almost encircled by the narrow wall-like ridges of Striding Edge and Swirral Edge—both walker's routes. Swirral Edge terminates in the little peak of Catchedicam, noted by Camden as one of the highest hills in England and included by Mackintosh in his list of shapely conical mountains. Professor Tyndall, the eminent Alpine mountaineer, contributed an account of a winter ascent of Helvellyn to the *Saturday Review* in 1859: 'a day of wonderous atmospheric effects, indeed we had scarcely seen anything grander among the Alps themselves'. Of recent years Helvellyn has become one of the centres of Lake District ski-ing; the local ski club has a hut and a diesel-engined ski-tow on the upper slopes. This sport has become increasingly popular all over the area during the last two decades and is available in most winters to anyone prepared to go high enough.

Eastwards now is Patterdale with Ullswater, the second largest lake. From here the Kirkstone Pass crosses to Troutbeck and Windermere, while further east lie the less rocky but more secluded Eastern Fells. Notable among the mountains is High Street, which has a Roman road running along the crest, while below it is Haweswater, impounded more recently as another water source for Manchester. Shap Fells continue the line of the high country right across to the Pennines, involving a stiff climb for the railway on the west coast route to Scotland. Long walks have been made from the Pennines to the Lake District across these connecting hills, notably in the 1950s an 80-mile trip from Grassington in Wharfedale to Langdale over the tops of many of the intervening hills in 36 hours.

The northern half of the 'wheel' is now behind us and we continue our journey round it circling southwards and westwards. Passing over Long Sleddale and Kentmere we reach Windermere, the largest of the lakes, set amidst attractive hills, lower and wooded. From the lake head four valleys branch into the mountains. Troutbeck runs north-ward and from it the Kirkstone Pass crosses to Patterdale. From a source near Dunmail Raise on the main road from Ambleside to Keswick, the River Rathay runs through the small lakes of Grasmere, the centre of Wordsworthland, and Rydal Water before joining Windermere at Water Head. Close by, the River Brathay, which has come down from the Langdales, also joins in. Great Langdale ends abruptly below the steep walls of the Langdale Pikes and Bowfell, the only exits being by the paths up Rossett Gill to Esk Hause and Wasdale and up Stake Pass to Borrowdale. Little Langdale farther south leads up to Wrynose Pass and the Three Shires Stone; beyond is the head of Dunnerdale. West of Windermere beyond the low hills of the Bannisdale Slates lies Coniston Water, recent scene of attempts on the world's water speed record. This is Lancashire. The county summit, the Coniston Old Man (2,633 feet), scarred on this side by mine workings, looks down on the other towards Dunnerdale and the Duddon River.

Two important mountains rise between the lakeless valleys of Dunnerdale and Eskdale. Harter Fell, a craggy pyramid, is said to be the only mountain in the whole district which requires the use of the hands to reach the summit. Much farther south and made of the same rocks as Skiddaw stands the isolated Black Combe, of which Words-worth wrote:

> . . . *from the summit of Black Combe (dread name derived*
> *from clouds and storm) the amplest range*
> *Of unobstructed prospect may be seen*
> *That British ground commands.*

The view on an exceptional day will certainly include, as well as the high peaks of the Lake District, those of Lancashire, Yorkshire, North Wales, the Isle of Man and South Scotland, while even Ireland may be visible.

The two valleys are joined at the head by Hard Knott Pass, originally a Roman road from the coast into the interior; near the summit is the Roman fort of Hard Knott Castle. Camden describes it as 'Hardknot, an high steepe mountaine, in the top whereof were discovered of late huge stones and foundations of a castle not without great wonder, considering it is so steepe and upright that one can hardly ascend to it.' The notion that there was a high mountain called Hard Knot persisted for many years. Gray spoke of 'Wrynose and Hardknot, two great mountains, rising above the rest', while even the usually accurate West mentions the 'overhanging cliff of Hardknot'.

Eskdale is another very pleasant valley—'second only to Borrowdale' says Haskett Smith, which runs up to the south side of Mickledore below the Scafells. There is a famous narrow-gauge railway in the valley. Somewhere, too, Hutchinson tells us are 'Doe Cragg and Earn Cragg, remarkable precipices, whose fronts are polished as marble, the one 160 perpendicular yards in height, the other 120 yards'; climbers have not yet located these splendid sounding cliffs.

We leave Eskdale by the Burnmoor Tarn path which crosses between the dull sides of Scafell and Wastwater Screes. Then suddenly we are back again above the chequer-board field pattern of Wasdale Head, the cirque of high mountains and the farms and the inn, which witnessed the birth of British rock climbing and have seen so much of its story. And we can echo once again the words of Wilkinson: 'Who would regret that once in his life he had come down to explore the wonders of Wast Water.'

It was here that the sport of rock climbing as we know it today began in the 1880s. During the middle years of the nineteenth century mountaineers who were then making history in the Alps used to come here mostly in the winter for recreation and to get such practice as they could by cutting steps up hard snow in the gullies and by walking across the fells. When they came in spring or summer it was again for the walking, diversified later by the ascents of relatively inaccessible major features such as Pillar Rock or Scafell Pinnacle. In 1881 the men who were to change all this met for the first time at Wasdale—Walter Parry Haskett Smith, then an undergraduate, and Frederick Bowring, a veteran explorer of the hills of Britain already in his sixties. Haskett Smith was a member of a reading party which, planning a month in the Lake District, had selected the region of darkest shading on the hachured map and so hit on Dan Tyson's inn at Wasdale Head; here Bowring was a frequent visitor. Bowring was not the sort of man to stick to paths or guidebook routes; in fact guidebooks were still more or less useless even for the crossing of the simplest of passes. He was accustomed to go wherever the straightforward use of hands and feet, what we now call scrambling, would take him. Haskett Smith later recalled this picture of him:

> Bowring was indifferent to weather and seldom did more to meet it than tying a sort of grey bandanna over a hat originally of hard felt, but softened by the lapse of years. His tall figure bore a long-tailed morning coat, probably the same which he wore in London, and in its pockets he kept an amazing assortment of loose fieldglasses, tobacco pipes, string, knives, sandwiches, maps and usually several books of foreign poetry.

The more energetic members of the University party found in him an inspiration for tackling unorthodox routes up and over the hill-sides. The vital influence was on the young Haskett Smith who learned that there could be real pleasure in climbing for its own sake—an energetic and exciting exercise giving a most intimate insight into the hills in all their moods.

He was back again the next year, this time with his brother, and in a nine-week stay began to do climbs of a standard which would still be regarded as rock climbing today. Many of the early routes were made up the clefts in the crags which are called gullies, partly because they provided obvious ways, which could be described and followed, partly because of the feeling of security that early climbers found inside the enclosing walls. The Alpine-trained climbers were not idle and they came in ever increasing numbers during the next few years to see what was really going on among these northern fells. They liked what they found and from their experience soon began to make their own contributions to the climbs. During this period the two groups gradually coalesced, the locals bringing the idea of climbing rocks for pleasure, the

Alpinists technical features such as ice axes and ropes, from their sort of mountaineering. We look back on 1886 as the year when the sport really arrived, Haskett Smith making in June the first ascent of the rock pinnacle of Napes Needle on the Wasdale face of Great Gable. He came over the summit of Great Gable late one afternoon and descended the full length of Needle Ridge to the foot of the Pinnacle:

> . . . the Needle itself had an attractive look about it. The main trouble lay in the cracks and crevices which were tightly packed with small stones flush with the surface of the slabs and thatched with slippery grass. The prospect from the shoulder was not encouraging. The Lingmell face of the top block was covered with a brown brittle lichen, which concealed whatever holds there might be, and if the top of the block were rounded, things looked hopeless. The only test of this was to throw up a stone and, if it stayed there, it would be a proof that the top was fairly flat. Diligent search revealed only two stones on the shoulder, one the size of a snuff-box, the other nearly as big as a brick. The little one bounded off and was lost; but the big one behaved better and encouraged me to follow it. There was no means of recording my visit except a small boss near the north edge of the stone round which my handkerchief was tied with my brick on top of it to keep it from being blown away . . . In the descent hanging by the hands from the top and feeling with the toes for the protuberance provided an anxious moment, but the rest went easily enough, though it must be confessed that it was an undoubted satisfaction to stand once more on solid ground below and look up at my handkerchief fluttering in the breeze.

The ascent of the Needle with its ferocious appearance of inaccessibility was a landmark and its association with Haskett Smith confirms and commemorates his responsibility for the very beginnings. The pinnacle was later (1890) described in a national magazine—the *Pall Mall Budget*—and this article did much to attract would-be climbers to the fells. Haskett Smith's own account was not published until nearly 30 years later.

In 1894 and 1895 came the first books on the new sport, written appropriately by Haskett Smith and describing climbing on rocks in many parts of England and Wales; indeed they remained the last word on some districts until the spate of literature in the post-1945 boom. Though Haskett Smith subsequently did little more for British climbing he survived to make a Jubilee ascent of the Needle in 1936.

18 *The Langdale P.*

At Easter, 1890, a new and more technically competent generation arrived in Wasdale in the shape of Owen Glynne Jones. He started slowly, but once into his stride, he made new climbs all over the place, describing them in a monumental work, *Rock Climbing in the English Lake District*, which appeared in 1897. Unfortunately an accident in the Alps robbed us of this great innovator in 1899 at the age of 32. We notice here two other men of the Lake District, friends of Jones, who played an outstanding part in the popularization of British mountains and climbing. These were the 'Keswick Brothers', Ashley and George Abraham, climbers and professional photographers, who took large cameras up mountains and rock climbs and brought back pictures which were widely published in their own books and elsewhere. Jones did much of his climbing with a 'strong arm' technique, using his unusual strength to swing up on the handholds rather than stepping up on the footholds. Thus his routes tended to follow the lines of gullies, cracks and chimneys rather than open rocks. Towards the end of his career he did seem to be developing into a climber of a more general type, tackling rock slabs where the hands are used primarily for balance and progress is made by correct use of the feet on very small holds; we shall never know what he might eventually have done. Instead the development of climbing on these lines fell, during the first years of this century, to Fred Botterill, a Yorkshireman, and Siegfried Herford, born in Wales, a scientist by profession. Significantly each of them had originally learned to climb, and currently kept himself in form on the gritstone outcrops of the Peak and the West Riding, and this really marks the beginning of the tremendous influence which these practice rocks were to have thenceforward on British climbing. Each of them made outstanding climbs on the great north face of Scafell on the Wasdale side of Mickledore, Botterill on a very exposed slab, since named after him, Herford on the so-called Central Buttress, where the overhanging Flake Crack required combined tactics and rope work which have a distinctly modern flavour.

A day was devoted to threading a rope loop behind a stone jammed high up in the crack below the upper overhang but repeated efforts to get higher failed so the party retired to Wasdale for the night. The next morning it was seen that the rope loop hanging from the chockstone showed signs of wear, and this was replaced without too much difficulty. 'We decided,' wrote the second man (G. S. Sansom) afterwards, 'that combined tactics would be necessary, and accordingly ran a second rope through the loop. Herford tied on one rope and I on another, whilst Gibson and Holland manipulated the respective ropes. I followed Herford closely up the crack and hung on to the loop whilst he used my shoulders as footholds. Directly he vacated them I climbed three feet higher and hung by my hands from the top of the chockstone, whilst he again employed me as footholds, which are most sorely needed at this point, for the crack is practically holdless and overhangs about twenty degrees. A minute or two of severe struggling and he reached the top—to the great joy of all members of the party.'

Central Buttress, recently described as 'by a long way the most important event in British rock climbing up to 1914', is a climb which has held its reputation for severity right up to the present day. During this period, too, the Fell and Rock Climbing Club of the English Lake District was formed by local enthusiasts to cater for men and women interested in walking and climbing hereabouts. Nowadays it has more than 1,000 members and is the biggest climbing club in these Islands.

Following the break of the First World War, with its great losses of manpower from all walks of life, climbing was slow to pick up, but by the mid-1920s new climbs of ever increasing standard were being put up all over the district by H. M. Kelly, George Bower, Fred Pigott and others. Specialized climbers' guidebooks describing the exact line of each route were brought out to a model first worked out by Kelly for Pillar Rock.

In the 1930s Maurice Linnell, A. T. Hargreaves and R. J. Birkett were prominent in the next generation of innovators. Lines on old crags continued to get harder, while new crags were opened up as obstacles formerly shunned such as steep, poor-quality rock and vegetation-covered rock came to be tackled. Typical of these was the wet, overhanging East Buttress of Scafell. Linnell's account of a first ascent here exhibits an aggressive outlook towards the use of pitons, which at that time were completely unacceptable to the majority of climbers:

> There was only one thing for it, and it was an eventuality for which I had come prepared. I inserted a piton in the little crack, and inserted it well and truly with a hammer. Nor was it only put there as a safeguard; by pulling it sideways, downwards, outwards, and upwards, and finally planting

a foot on it, I was able, with a struggle, to reach a little ledge. I offer no apologies; those who prefer to climb the place unaided are cordially invited to remove the piton and do so.

Now only 30 years later no leader of new climbs could manage without them.

Immediately after the Second World War R. J. Birkett continued to make new climbs, as did newcomers, such as W. Peascod and A. R. Dolphin. Now in the last 20 years interest in climbing has spread at a remarkable rate. More and more experts have come to the fore capable of doing all the hardest climbs. Standards rise continuously and smaller crags off the beaten track have been in their turn assaulted and charted. Just as in Snowdonia, the fiercest climbs are described in a nonchalant language which gives no hint that most of us would be unable even to leave the ground on them, let alone make any upward progress. Here is just a little of the pioneer account by Paul Ross of a climb on the Castle Rock of Triermain in St John's Vale, which he called Rigor Mortis because it was rather stiff:

> Up to the left I noticed another slight projection, but it was not until after much strenuous swinging and chipping that this became suitable for a single line sling. Transferring myself to this sling—my perch for the next hour—was no mean feat as it needed very little encouragement to roll off. Eventually I managed to jam a piton into a wide crack to steady myself and started to hammer at a knife edge up to the right, trying to find a weakness to make some sort of spike on which to hang yet another sling. After a great deal of banging a chunk flew off, just missing Bill, but leaving a beautiful sharp spike. I now lifted the jammed piton (which was no longer necessary), out of the crack and, using a stiff sling, managed to hook it over the spike and transfer myself; I then felt a lot safer. About 5 feet above this I succeeded in knocking in what looked like a secure piton . . .

With the large numbers of straightforward mountain ascents and pass crossings which are available, walking is a popular pastime; indeed, as we have said, only the walker can cross direct from valley to valley and only the walker can see the real heart of the mountains. It is not surprising therefore that a tradition of long-distance walking should have grown up in such a compact and suitable area. Marathon walks round the peaks began about 100 years ago and the numbers of peaks, and of miles, and of feet of ascent and descent, done in one expedition have been increasing steadily ever since. The first outstanding figure was A. W. Wakefield, who in 1905 did 59 miles and 23,500 feet in 22 hours 7 minutes; in the 1920s Eustace Thomas, aided by Wakefield, increased this to $66\frac{1}{2}$ miles and 25,500 feet within 24 hours. Now the Rules of the Game settled down to—covering as many as possible 2,000-foot summits inside 24 hours, starting and finishing at the same point. In 1932 R. B. Graham beat this time doing 42 mountains in 23 hours 39 minutes, K. Heaton improved it again in 1961 (82 miles, 31,000 feet, 51 mountains in 22 hours 13 minutes) and finally in 1963, E. Beard, who already held the record for the Welsh 3,000s, managed 56 mountains in 23 hours 35 minutes. This is, of course, cross-country running of an extremely high standard. Similarly cross-country runners dominate the annual Fell Race, in which competitors are given their first objective at the start and further objectives as the race goes on; thus no one knows the exact course beforehand and there is some scope for selection of the best route by map or 'eye for country'.

Scafell Pike has to be climbed by those different stalwarts who seek to visit the highest points of England, Scotland and Wales in one expedition, but this is a feat which demands more skill in motoring than in mountain climbing. The ordinary hill walker will be satisfied with something less ambitious than all this—the 3,000-foot mountains in one expedition, a round of a valley head and so forth.

Before leaving the subject of records there is one delightfully different which deserves mention: T. Tyson and C. Dodgson have bathed in every one of the 463 mountain tarns of Lakeland!

SIX

Ireland—General,
Leinster and Munster

'The land of Ireland', wrote Fynes Moryson in 1600, 'is uneven, mountainous, soft, watery, woody, and open to winds and floods of rain, and so fenny as it hath bogs upon the very tops of mountains, not bearing man or beast, but dangerous to pass, and such bogs are frequent all over Ireland.'

Three-quarters of the country lies below 500 feet and only 5 per cent is above 1,000 feet. Broadly, it is saucer-shaped—a comparatively flat midland plain centred on Athlone with almost all the hills and mountains close to the coastline. In the east are the Wicklow and Leinster Mountains, to the south the Comeraghs and the Galtees, in the south-west the serried hills of Cork and Kerry, where Carrauntual (3,414 feet) in the group called Macgillycuddy's Reeks is the summit of the country. The line of hills continues northwards through the Burren of Clare, the Connemara district of Galway, Mayo, Sligo and Donegal; finally the hills of Northern Ireland in Antrim and the Mountains of Mourne complete the circle.

Giraldus, whose accounts of his Welsh travels we have already considered, came to Ireland in 1183 and 1185. His book, *Topographica Hibernica*, has been described as indicating that the national sport of spinning yarns to cross-channel correspondents is at least 800 years old. He was convinced that the layout of the mountains was quite different—'on the whole', he says, 'the land is low lying on all sides and along the coast, but towards the centre it rises up very high to many hills and even fine mountains'. We can perhaps excuse him because it was long held, at least up to the seventeenth century, that the Slieve Blooms, way off in the centre of the country, were the highest in the land.

The separation between Ireland and Great Britain only took place in comparatively recent geological times and there is an obvious continuity of rock formations on either side of the Irish Sea. Thus the Highlands of Scotland continue in the mountains of Donegal, Mayo and Connemara and the Southern Uplands in the hills of Armagh and Down and the Mourne Mountains, but the area corresponding to the central Lowlands is overlain by extensive lava sheets in County Antrim. In southern Ireland many geological features, such as the continuation of the limestone and Old Red Sandstone strata, resemble those of South Wales over the sea, though Wales has no parallel to the granite Wicklow Mountains. Beneath the central plain is a vast stretch of Mountain Limestone which reaches the coast at various gaps in the mountain ring. Much of the land is covered by glacial debris in the form of boulder clay (it was completely covered during the Ice Age) and by peat. This curious vegetable blanket, as it has been called, occupies one-seventh of the whole land area, covering mountain groups like the Comeraghs, the Galtees and the Sperrins with an average depth of five feet and reaching an average depth of no less than 18 feet over the central plain. The peats, used extensively as fuel, are said to be past their optimum and now in the process of decay.

The ring mountains show a number of contrasting rock types— granite in the Wicklows, the Mournes and in Donegal, Old Red Sandstone in Kerry, the Galtees and the Silvermine Mountains, Mountain Limestone in Clare, Sligo and Fermanagh, quartzite in the Sperrins and in Donegal, Mayo and Connemara, basalt in Antrim and so on. In conjunction with a generally moist and often mild climate these lead to a wide variety of mountain form and character. The eminent mountaineer, Geoffrey Young, whose knowledge of the mountains of Ireland was second to none, has written of them:

> To look upon, there are no more lovely mountains: as we can see them from Marble Head in the north, back over the brown lift of bogland to the dark cone of Errigal; or from Mizzen Head in the south, back over the lake of wild swans to the lilac Kerry hills; or from western Slyne Head where it lies far out in the Atlantic, back over the miles of white sand and black rocks and low green dunes, to the Connemara Pins: mountains as boldly sculptured upon the grey sky as are the Euganean hills seen from Venice, but even more impressive in their remoteness upon this outermost landfall.

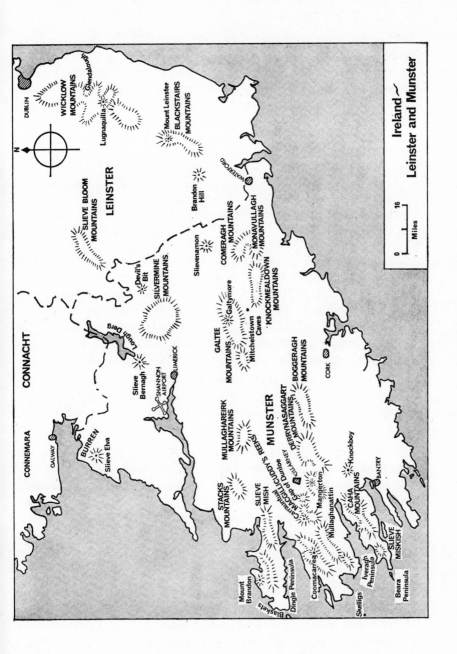

Ireland ~
Leinster and Munster

Miles
0 ___ 16

CONNACHT

CONNEMARA

GALWAY

BURREN

Slieve Elva

Lough Derg

Slieve Bernagh

SHANNON AIRPORT

LIMERICK

STACKS MOUNTAINS

SLIEVE MISH

MULLAGHAREIRK MOUNTAINS

MUNSER

GALTE MOUNTAINS

Galtymore

Mitchelstown Caves

KNOCKMEALDOWN MOUNTAINS

BOGGERAGH MOUNTAINS

CORK

DERRYNASAGGART MOUNTAINS

MACGILLICUDDY'S REEKS

Carrauntohill

Gap of Dunloe

KILLARNEY

Mangerton

Mullaghanattin

CAHA MOUNTAINS

Knockboy

BANTRY

SLIEVE MISKISH

Mount Brandon

Blaskets

Dingle Peninsula

Coomacarrea

Iveragh Peninsula

Skelligs

Beara Peninsula

DUBLIN

WICKLOW MOUNTAINS

Glendalough

Lugnaquilla

Mount Leinster

BLACKSTAIRS MOUNTAINS

Brandon Hill

LEINSTER

SLIEVE BLOOM MOUNTAINS

Devil's Bit

SILVERMINE MOUNTAINS

Slievenamon

COMERAGH MOUNTAINS

MONAVULLAGH MOUNTAINS

WATERFORD

123

There are views northward from among the hills of County Mayo, in which the coastal sea has the restless stillness of arctic green ice, frosted with wave crests, and the rock islands stand high above it, castles of silver-blue cloud. I have driven westward through the Pins, on summer evenings when their whole solidity of rock outline and surface was penetrated and transfused with a liquid gold light. They glowed semi-transparently about us, luminous shapes so unsubstantial that it seemed the going down of the sunlight must dissipate them like wraiths of mist. There is some quality in slanting Irish light at evening which transforms all it falls upon into poetry, the vision of a lovelier earth. Just as the sound of music has the power to sublimate what we are reading or thinking, this light can throw a halo about every object and happening.

As usual no one knows who first climbed these mountains, though in two cases there are illustrious claimants to the honour. In 441 St Patrick himself spent 40 days on the summit of Croagh Patrick, County Mayo, in prayer and fasting, during which, or just after which, he expelled snakes and poisonous reptiles from Ireland for ever; Brendan, the Navigator, built an oratory on the summit of Mount Brandon, County Kerry, which he either lived in or often visited in the days before he set out on his adventurous voyage westwards to America. Both these mountains are now places of pilgrimage.

There are of course other climbing accounts from later ages, for example, Crohaun in the Comeraghs, of which Dr Charles Smith wrote in 1745:

> On the sides of this chain there are many horrid precipices and steep declivities, with large naked rocks, not only towards the tops, but also in most of their other crags, till one descends into the vallies, where considerable chips or parings lie in prodigious heaps, consisting of stones intermixed with sand and gravel and sometimes of large rocks and broken fragments. Thus, in time, these mountains are wasted, no doubt from their being exposed to the vast quantities of hail and snow which fall on them.

In the same century (1796) Mangerton, near Killarney, was climbed for the view by Le Chevalier de la Tocnaye, who was touring the country. By now Killarney was a popular tourist centre and ascents of local mountains were made more and more frequently in the ensuing years; round this time, too, all doubts were resolved and Carrauntual accepted as the highest point in the land.

When W. P. Haskett Smith produced his pioneering book *Rock Climbing in the British Isles* in 1895 he commissioned a section on Ireland from H. C. Hart, a Dublin botanist, who was a prodigious walker. Hart once walked for a wager from Dublin to the summit of Lugnaquilla, the highest point in the Wicklow Mountains, and back inside 24 hours, a total distance of 75 miles over hills most of the way. His account of Ireland was for walkers, scramblers and nature lovers and made little mention of rock climbing. Later, after the turn of the century, a few climbs were done, but the explorers were unusually unenterprising and concluded, in the words of a contemporary article, that 'rock suitable for serious climbing is almost entirely lacking'. The hiking and youth hostelling movement of the 1930s sent many young people out on to the hills for the first time, but in spite of climbing developments elsewhere Ireland continued to lag far behind. It was not until the great upsurge period which began in 1945 that real progress was made; an Irish Mountaineering Club was at last formed and climbs began to spring up all over the country. Now all stages of rock climbing development took place simultaneously—old-fashioned gully and ridge climbs sometimes of moderate standards alongside face climbs which demanded the utmost of modern techniques. The chief climbing areas are the granites of Wicklow, Donegal and the Mournes; many possibilities remain.

There are eleven 3,000-foot mountains in Ireland and these were ascended by a north-of-England party in a period of four days in 1962. Lugnaquilla fell on the first day, Galtymore on the second, the eight 3,000ers in Macgillycuddy's Reeks on the third and Brandon on the fourth. They used a car of course to travel from group to group. There is little doubt that this time could be shortened by anyone who thought it worth the trouble; one day, too, it will be done without a car. We have to notice an historic ascent of Carrauntual in 1937, when a party of four reached the summit by way of Scafell Pike and Snowdon, having left the summit of Ben Nevis 26 hours before. Cars and an aeroplane played their parts in this extraordinary feat.

Though the caves at Mitchelstown, Co. Tipperary, had been known for many years, the real story of caving in Ireland began with the visit of E. A. Martel, the noted French speleologist, in 1895. A steady stream of parties from Great Britain has followed and some spectacular discoveries have been made. The principal caving areas are Sligo—Fermanagh—Leitrim, where Noon's Hole is the deepest in Ireland, and County Clare, where Poulnagollum is the country's most extensive cave system. Very considerable possibilities await the ardent cave explorer.

*   *   *   *   *

The province of Leinster comprises 12 counties in eastern and southern Ireland. The outstanding mountain group is the Leinster Chain, a 70-mile range of granite hills which runs from Kildare and Dublin, through Wicklow and along the Carlow–Wexford border to finish in Kilkenny. One mountain, Lugnaquilla (3,039 feet), rises above 3,000 feet; about 50 exceed 2,000 feet. There are worthy hill groups in Laois, the Slieve Blooms, and in Louth, the Carlingford Mountains, otherwise there is no other land above the 1,000-foot contour.

The Wicklow Mountains—the biggest granite block in the British Isles—were formed when a huge molten mass rose up below the local flat beds of slaty rocks, forcing them into a long, domed ridge. The upper rocks, metamorphosed in the process to schists, were later removed from the tops by denudation, leaving the country very much as we see it today—a long line of rounded peat-covered granite hills with schists and quartzites below. The denudation was not absolutely complete and in fact the highest summits of Lugnaquilla and Table Mountain are small remnants of the original rock still standing above the granite. The length of the range is traversed by the Military Road, running from Rathfarnham near Dublin to Aughavannagh far to the south, which was built to hold down the country after the troubles of 1798.

As we move southwards from Dublin the hills steadily increase in height until the highest point in the county, Kippure (2,475 feet), with its television mast, is reached on the Wicklow border. Away to the east at Glencullen extensive remains of the Irish Elk, over 100 individuals, were found in the filled-up lake of Ballybetagh. This magnificent animal, long since extinct, had an antler span of 11½ feet; though found as far afield as Greece and Russia, here in Ireland it seemed to attain maximum size and numbers. Nearby the Dublin-to-Enniskerry road passes through a narrow rocky gorge, the Scalp, where some climbs have been made. Beyond Kippure a pass crosses the range at Sally Gap from the upper Liffey Valley in the west to that of the Annamoe River in the east. A few miles from Sally Gap the Dargle River tumbles over a 300-foot crag of schist and gneiss at the well-known Powerscourt Waterfall. In 1895 this was the scene of one of the earliest climbs in Ireland. It was a hard winter and the cliffs by the fall were plastered with ice and snow; ropes and ice axes were used and the climb continued in a blizzard to the top of Djouce (2,384 feet) above.

The Annamoe runs south-eastwards from Sally Gap. In the words of a writer in 1801:

> A very slender stream proceeds to Lough Tay, which forms a beautiful basin of about three miles in circumference, situated at the bottom of most stupendous and craggy mountains, one of which presents a most formidable appearance of an inaccessible precipice. On the other side, it seems overhung by a bold and rugged mass, with mountains upon mountains piled around. Passing from the Gap by a narrow defile, on the summit of this mountain, with the lough immediately below you, you are astonished at the perception in the bosom of this rugged crater, of a polished surface of the most verdant meads, interspersed with a variety of the leafy tribe. Curiosity is on the wing to form a conjecture of the friendly hand which has relieved with such delightful scenery, this forbidding waste. The enchantment is fully explained, when you recognise, in opening on the view of Luggala, the hand of a Latouche.

The 'inaccessible precipice' is the great granite crag of Luggala, which lies in the Guinness family estate; an early rock climb was made here by Page Dickinson in 1907. There were further explorations during the upsurge after 1945, but it was not until 1959 that the overhanging main face gave a magnificent climb of very high standard to an Anglo-Irish party. The key to the climb was a hand traverse, that is one with hands on the rock and feet swinging in space, at the end of which the leader had to swing up and round a corner without knowing what he would find there. In the words of his second, he moved round 'with a vicious swing, looking as if he was riding a rearing horse; then he managed to pull up with his last remaining bit of strength'. Round the corner there was something climbable and all was well. On the other side of the Military road there are numerous 2,000-foot mountains including Mullaghcleevaun (2,788 feet), 'the summit with the cradle', the second mountain of Leinster, and Thonelagee, 'back to the wind'.

Another road crosses the range at Wicklow Gap and runs down on the east side to the lower end of Glendalough, 'the valley of the two lakes', famous for its extensive ecclesiastical ruins, said to be among the oldest Christian buildings in Europe. St Kevin, who came here in the sixth century to live the life of a hermit, built the first of the churches on the south side of the upper lake and subsequently a monastic city grew up around it. The ruins of seven churches remain. Here too is one of the finest specimens of the round towers characteristic of the Irish scene. These are generally of the ninth century and were sited near ecclesiastical buildings to serve as watch-towers, belfries or store-houses. The height varied from 50 to 120 feet and the entrance, always well above ground level, was presumably reached by retractable ladder. The Glendalough tower is 110 feet in height and 52 feet in circumference.

Giraldus (1185) tells a strange tale of these hills:

> Shortly before the coming of the English into the island a calf that was half a man was born in the mountains round Glendalough . . . It spent nearly a year with the other calves, following its mother and feeding on her milk, and then, because it had more of the human than the beast, was transferred to the society of men.

'Which conclusively proves', adds Ciaran Mac an Fhaili in *Irish Mountaineering* (1960), 'that the Wicklow Mountains could boast an Abominable Cowman centuries before the Himalayas produced the Abominable Snowman.'

Throughout the ages travellers have been making the pilgrimage to Glendalough; now others come for a quite different reason for this is one of the outstanding rock climbing centres of Ireland. Above the upper lake are steep vegetation-covered cliffs of schist which are of little use, but higher up the valley there are fine granite crags on the north side on Camaderry. The first climb here was only made in 1948 yet two years later the lessons of modern technique had been so well absorbed that high standard routes, using pitons and the whole up-to-date paraphernalia, were already being made. Here, for example, is an incident in the first ascent of Cuchulainn Groove, described by Peter Kenny:

> Finally, Frank once more edged upwards slowly and carefully, sometimes jamming, sometimes using a lay-back, until he reached a point about 30 feet above the bulge. Here some relief was obtained, and a psychological running belay on a piton was constructed. Moving up again Frank tried to stand on the piton, but, immediately, it swivelled downwards in its vertical crack, and only by a convulsive contortion was a fall averted. Continuing for another few feet, he reached a wrinkle at the apex of the slab on the right, and moved out of the groove on to this. Then, kicking off his right shoe, he performed a delicate step on to a sloping and damp foothold, from which it was possible to obtain a hold for the hands on a steep slope of vegetation. While he was making the last movement, the piton belay had come out completely, but, fortunately, Frank was too engrossed to notice this.

From Laragh the Military Road crosses the hills to Drumgoff in Glenmalure, from which Lugnaquilla can be readily climbed. On southwards rise a mass of lesser hills crossed by several main roads; then beyond Newtonbarry rise the Blackstairs Mountains (Mount Leinster, 2,610 feet) which continue along the Carlow–Wexford border. The name is said to come from the risers of dark rocks which stretch up towards the summit of Blackstairs itself on the west side. This is granite once again and the main summits are flat and boggy. Westwards beyond the River Barrow the isolated Brandon Hill, the highest point of County Kilkenny, marks the end of the chain.

Shared between the counties of Laois and Offaly is the 20-mile grass and peat ridge of the Slieve Blooms. These hills rise from the plains in comparative isolation and thus have an apparent importance out of proportion with their height. The topmost point, Ard Erin, 'the height of Ireland', is only 1,734 feet, yet until the seventeenth century it was thought to be the highest in the land. Here rise the three great rivers Suir, Nore and Barrow. The remaining counties in the south of Leinster have no major hills. Kildare shares some of the foothills of the Wicklow Mountains, but is otherwise markedly flat. Longford, Meath and Westmeath reach to only 800–950 feet. One considerable hill group remains and that so far north as to be almost a part of Ulster. In the northern corner of Louth is the Cooley

Peninsula, where the rocky Carlingford Mountains, made of gabbro, look across Carlingford Lough to the Mountains of Mourne. Slieve Foye, the highest point, is 1,935 feet.

*　　*　　*　　*　　*

Six counties in the south and west—namely, Waterford, Cork, Tipperary, Kerry, Limerick and Clare—form the province of Munster. The chief mountain groups are the Comeraghs, Knockmealdowns and Galtees on the borders of the first three counties, the high hills in the west of Cork and Kerry, the Silvermines and the Devil's Bit on the Tipperary–Limerick border and the limestone hills of Clare.

The Comeraghs in Waterford are a plateau of Old Red Sandstone with horizontal strata of conglomerates and grits. Round the edges are glacier-worn hollows backed by steep cliffs, such as Coumshingaun, 'the hollow of the ants', which lies below Fauscoum (2,597 feet), the highest point of the range. Though they all agree on the height various authorities differ over the actual name of this peak; one calls it Knockaunpeebra, actually elsewhere and 200 feet lower, another Knockanaffrin, elsewhere but only 100 feet lower. Certainly Fauscoum sounds more like a hollow than a mountain. A short distance to the north is Crotty's Lake, named after a highwayman who lived thereabouts, hanged in Waterford in 1742. The Comeraghs provide some of the finest ridge walks in Ireland with plenty of rock scenery and a little climbing. Southwards the Monavullagh Mountains extend the line of the hills almost to the sea at Dungarvan. To the north beyond the Suir the isolated hill of Slievenamon gives splendid views back to the Comeraghs and over the wide surrounding plains.

West of the Comeraghs and the Monavullaghs come the Knockmealdown Mountains (2,608 feet), the name derived, we are told, with charming lack of certainty, either from 'bare brown mountain' or from 'Maoldomhnach's Mountain'. They take the form of a simple ridge running from east to west, heathy and with only a little bare rock. A main road pass, the Vee Road, crosses the centre of the range at over 1,000 feet enabling the motorist to share these hills in a way denied to him in the Comeraghs or the Galtees. On the southern slopes is the Trappist monastery of Mount Melleray.

To the north-west the Galtee Mountains, 'mountains of the woods', said to be Ireland's finest inland group, reach 3,018 feet at Galtymore (sometimes called Dawson's Table). On this, the eighth mountain of the country, a large stone cross, erected in 1932, commemorates the fifteen-hundredth anniversary of the landing of St Patrick, or, some say, is a memorial to the local guerillas of the 1920s. The range, which is of Silurian slate capped with Old Red Sandstone conglomerates, gives a fine ridge walk of 15 miles from Cahir on the Suir to Mitchelstown. The tops are turf, heather and peat, while on the flanks, particularly on the north side above the Glen of Aherlow, are rocky corries with lakes, notably Loughs Muskry, Curra and Diheen, having great crags above. The botanist can find much of interest hereabouts. H. C. Hart, who usually did his climbing in search of plants, wrote:

> Should the climber get pounded here (as not seldom happens) let him beware of undue haste. A mouthful of food has a wonderful effect in steadying the nerves. The holds are often sods of dubious security, and the Muskry precipices, though they can be traversed in all directions are the severest among the Galtees.

There are two famous caves, known as Mitchelstown Caves, near Ballyporeen on the Cahir–Mitchelstown road, lying in the limestone trough between the Galtees and the Knockmealdowns. The Old Cave, visited and described by Arthur Young in 1777, into which the explorer must descend by ladder, has one of the largest chambers in the country, 400 feet long and 100 feet wide. Some of the finest formations were removed and sold by starving local peasants during the famine of 1847–8. The New Cave, first discovered in 1833, is a show cave with 1½ miles of passages. At Kilcolman Castle, south-west of the Galtees, Edmund Spenser, the Elizabethan poet, lived for an eight-year period during which he wrote the first three books of the *Faerie Queene*.

In the west of Counties Cork and Kerry are the highest and most attractive mountains in Ireland. The unusual combination of high mountains and rocky coastline is only to be matched in these Islands along the west coast of Scotland or in the Hebrides. There is one important difference, however. While large tracts of Scotland have been cleared of crofts and houses, leaving behind a lonely land,

Ireland is inhabited over much of its countryside. Here we have a classic example of what are known as rias, long narrow bays arising from relative change of level between sea and land in an area of roughly parallel ridges and furrows. The walls of the original valleys have become the coastline, with more resistant rocks forming islands. Here there are four prominent peninsulas running from north-east to south-west separated by long arms of the sea. The most southerly, which has no name, lies south of Bantry Bay and terminates in the headlands of Sheep's and Mizzen. Beyond Bantry Bay, a famous anchorage, is the narrow Beara Peninsula ending at Dursey Island, then the Kenmare River, then the broad Iveragh Peninsula, followed by Dingle Bay and finally Dingle Peninsula, with offshore the Blasket Islands, the part of Europe closest to America.

The nameless southerly peninsula is divided into two by the lesser inlet of Dunmanus Bay, south of which Mount Gabriel (1,339 feet) is the highest hill. This rises above the tiny harbour of Schull and commands a view over miles of coast and seascape to Cape Clear and Fastnet lighthouse. Between Dunmanus and Bantry Bays the hills are lesser but the roads across are splendid viewpoints for the ranges of hills in the Beara Peninsula on the north side of the Bay.

The road to Bantry from Macroom in the upper valley of the Lee runs through the impressive gorge-like Pass of Keimaneigh between Shehy Mountain to the south and a range which culminates in Knockboy (2,321 feet) to the north. Close by is the mountain-girt lake of Gougane Barra, 'St Finbarr's rock cleft', where the saint lived on an island in the sixth century. This is the source of the Lee which flows through extensive hydro works to the sea at Cork. To the west of Knockboy is the Kenmare to Glengarriff road, crossing from Cork into Kerry through the 200-yard Turner's Rock Tunnel. This is the beginning of the Beara Peninsula and beyond are the Caha Mountains. Glengarriff, on an inlet in the north corner of Bantry Bay, is sheltered on all sides except the south; the climate is mild even in winter and Mediterranean-type plants flourish amid a profusion of rocks. A few miles away the isolated Sugarloaf, Slieve na Goill, 'the misty hill', reaches 1,887 feet. Farther west the range is crossed at the Healy Pass by a road completed only in 1931, which gives the motorist another magnificent view of mountain and sea. Hungry Hill (2,251 feet) above Ardrigole is the highest point in the Caha Mountains. At the end of the Peninsula the Slieve Miskish Mountains rise to 2,044 feet at Maulin; Bere Haven to the south was abandoned as a base by the Royal Navy as recently as 1938. The rocks are all sandstones and, while some promising climbing crags have been reported hereabouts, hardly any exploration has yet taken place.

We cross now from the sea cliffs of Dursey Island in the extreme west of Beara to the western tip of Iveragh where the Skelligs, the peaks of great sea-bed mountains, rise eight miles off Bolus Head. Little Skellig is a breeding place for gannets; Great Skellig, 714 feet of grits and shales, has a lighthouse and ruins of an early Christian monastery. On the mainland the road girdling the coast of the peninsula from Killorglin to Kenmare is known as the Ring of Kerry and gives a round of about 100 miles from Killarney.

There are three prominent mountain groups. North of the minor road from Waterville through the Ballaghasheen Pass to Glencar a line of summits runs north-westwards, of which the highest is Coomacarrea (2,541 feet). An outstanding feature here is the series of four great cooms on the north-east flanks of the ridge; the largest is called Coomasaharn. The moderate western slopes have a peat covering which runs right up to the summits and in places even forms a cornice overhanging the eastern precipices. South of Ballaghasheen and west of the Ballaghbeama Pass (another very impressive gorge) is a group topped by Mullaghanattin (2,539 feet), 'the mountain of the gorse'. At the western end of these hills above Castlecove is the circular Staigue Fort, believed to be 2,000 years old.

The main ridge of Macgillycuddy's Reeks runs from west to east. Facing north-west to Glencar, Carrauntual (3,414 feet), 'the inverted reaping hook', the highest point of the group, of Kerry and of Ireland, rises at the head of Coomloughra flanked by Caher to the west and Beenkeragh (3,314 feet) to the north. East of Carrauntual the ridge runs on to Knock na Chuillion round Hag's Glen, the head of the Gaddagh River. The path from this glen to the ridge is called the Devil's Ladder. Hart describes climbing Carrauntual by this route on an occasion when thick mist covered the lower slopes; he had the rare and delightful experience of emerging above cloud level a short distance below the summit:

Above was a clear blue sky, and peering out of the dense white snowlike bed of mist Caher and Brandon (the latter 30 miles to the north-west, the former not a mile away) alone were visible—a never-to-be-forgotten sight, which seemed shut out entirely from earthly considerations.

The 'finest ridge walk in Ireland' lies eastwards from Knock na Chuillion with crags and great cliffs on the north side. There are four more 3,000-foot points before the ridge ends abruptly in steep cliffs at the deep-cut Gap of Dunloe (795 feet), famous beauty spot where all the worst features of tourism await to assail the unwary. This is an offshoot from the organized tourism of Killarney, which capitalizes to the utmost the justifiably great renown of its scenery. There seems little reason at the present time to differ from the pithy description of 50 years ago—'a tout-ridden paradise'. The local guides know little or nothing of the mountains and it is easy to escape their ministrations by turning uphill, which is what we will do forthwith!

The main peaks of the Reeks are hidden from Killarney by the somewhat lower, but extensive, Purple, Tomies and Shehy Mountains. South of the town a big area of moorland and mountain reaches 2,756 feet at Mangerton, 'the hairy one'. This is an easy ascent and a good viewpoint. The Devil's Punchbowl near the summit is a small lake set in a deep hollow, once thought to be the crater of an extinct volcano. Lesser mountains, the Derrynasaggart and the Boggeragh, stretch eastwards for many miles almost to Mallow.

Here we cross the Blackwater and turn back westwards via the Mullaghareirk Mountains and the Stacks Mountains and so to Dingle, the last of the Kerry peninsulas. The Slieve Mish Mountains stretch from Tralee to the southern coast near Anascaul. Baurtregaum (2,796 feet), 'the summit of the three hollows', is the highest point of this long range of smooth-sided hills. Farther on at over 2,000 feet on Caherconree is a fine promontory fort. The central hills between the Anascaul–Tralee road and the Connor Pass reach 2,713 feet at Beenoskee. This pass carries one of the highest main roads in Ireland and gives fine views over both sides of the hills and of the mass of Brandon to the north.

Mount Brandon (3,127 feet), first climbed by St Brendan long, long ago, is now famous as a place of pilgrimage; it is recorded, for instance, that 20,000 people climbed it in one day in 1868 under the guidance of a Dr Moriarty. On the east side are some huge crags and at least one climb has been done. The ridge terminates, beyond a final peak bearing the oriental-sounding name of Masatiompan, in tremendous sea cliffs. In Lough Bawn, Hart tells us,

> . . . lives the enormous carrabuncle. It appears fitfully at night, glittering like silver in the water with gold and silver and precious stones hanging to it galore. It is partly covered with shells, which are lined with gold. Upon one occasion several men went to the lake at night and dived in oilskins to catch this valuable monster. They did not catch him; but pearl mussels, no doubt shed from the carrabuncle, are found in the lake.

Geoffrey Young held the Brandon district in high esteem.

> 'Mountains,' he said, 'have character and we can remember them by their personality as we can great men . . . Mount Brandon stands above a most singular coast. Nature had her practice grounds where she experimented in form. She made the mistake, to my mind, of experimenting with lime-stone in far too many of her mountain modellings. But here or there we come upon regions of hill and cliff where the material has lent itself to bold fash-ioning, and where we may find in mountain line and mass the original of every type of human architecture. Upon the Kerry coast, for instance, it is almost startling to come upon the fantastic, often asymmetrical and in all respects modernistic shapes with which she has been experimenting . . . Above this disarray, in continual mist, and with its seaward precipices echoing monotonously the thunder of the Atlantic, Mount Brandon towers fabulously. It is as it were the finished dome, surmounting the litter and jettison of all that went into its creation. It is built as a beacon for the sea, on the edge of the last and first land.'

Mount Eagle stands in isolation at the west end of the peninsula; Dunmore Head below is the most westerly point of the mainland, the Blasket Islands offshore the most westerly point of Europe. These are more sea-bed mountains. Great Blasket, which is nearest, rises to 961 feet; farther out some of the small islands are remarkably steep, notably Tearaght, with its lighthouse, and Inishtooskert.

The next group of Munster hills is far away in northern Tipperary, beside the River Shannon. These are the Silvermine Mountains, once a source of silver and still worked for zinc and lead. Keeper Hill (2,279 feet) is the highest. To the north-east Devil's Bit Mountain rises close to Templemore. It is named after a remarkable gap, left when the Devil took a bite from the peak. Finding this morsel far from tasty, he ejected it on to the plains nearby—thus forming the Rock of Cashel. Alas for this romantic story, it is sad to record that, while the Devil's Bit is sandstone, the Rock of Cashel is limestone— in fact an incredible metamorphosis.

Across the Shannon is Clare, almost entirely limestone country with Slieve Bernagh (1,746 feet) above Killaloe the county summit. But the really startling limestone scenery is in the north-west in the district looking over to Galway, known as the Burren, 'great rock'. E. A. Baker, the noted caver, describing his first visit wrote:

> It was to this wilderness of stone that in the bad old days they used to drive evicted Catholics, a district pithily described by one of Cromwell's officers as not having 'water enough to drown a man, trees enough to hang a man, or earth enough to bury a man'. Geologists liken it to the Karst, the desolate limestone plateau north of Trieste, where the clint formation has its most extensive and savage development. The land, if 'land' is the word for it, is let at 1½d. an acre, and the poor beasts have a hard job to get his money's worth for the farmer from the few inches of browsing that come up through the cracks. Right, left, in front, as far as eye could see, stretched a pavement of naked limestone, the stoniest waste in the British Isles.

The area is particularly rich in unusual plant life due, says R. L. Praeger, to an abundance of moisture combined with good drainage, mild climate and the shelter given by the clints in the limestone pavement. There are prehistoric remains also and fine sea cliffs. It is, of course, caving country. Slieve Elva, the highest point of the Burren, shows the rock formations characteristic of the English caving areas— the hill is capped with Millstone Grit, resting on a layer of Yoredale shales, with a massive bed of limestone below. Streams on the upper strata sink into the rock where the limestone joins the shale. The limestone is pitted with potholes and swallets and, lower down, are the risings where the water reappears. Poulnagollum, on the east side of Slieve Elva, first entered by E. A. Baker and H. E. Kentish in 1912, has over four and a half miles of passages. Many others have been investigated and there is still scope for new discoveries and explorations.

20 Clifden and the Twelve
Co. Ga

SEVEN

Connacht and Ulster

Connacht comprises the counties of Galway, Mayo, Sligo, Leitrim and Roscommon and here again we find distinctive mountain groups around the coastline giving way to flat plains inland. Thus Roscommon, wholly in the interior, has no considerable mountains; the county summit of 1,385 feet is on the Leitrim border.

There are fine mountains in the Connemara district of Galway between Lough Corrib and the sea. Glen Inagh to the north of Recess separates the quartzite Twelve Bens (Benbaun, 2,395 feet) from the gneiss and quartzite Maamturk Mountains (Maamturk, 2,307 feet). The Twelve Bens occupy a circular area some six miles in diameter with Benbaun sited centrally and the remaining peaks, many of striking conical form, rising in a series of radiating ridges. This, Hart tells us, is 'the heart of some of the loveliest scenery in the world, full of varied and interesting scrambles, and botanically pre-eminently the richest in mountain plants in Connacht'. Of recent years climbers have found something more than scrambles and some long and interesting routes have been worked out. These mountains, like so many others in moist lake-strewn terrain, have other defences than the mere difficulties of the rock, as here described by Brighid MacCall:

> . . . Three of us did Carrot Ridge, its 900 feet of 'difficult' standard raised to 'extremely severe' by the midges which accompanied us all the way. We had to climb in bright hot sunlight with sleeves rolled down and Anorak hoods up to try and ward off the nightmare swarm that beat against us like rain. We sat at the belay points with scarves over our faces, smoking incessantly and, in my case, nearly in tears of frustration and rage. But, despite all precautions, we got bitten . . .

Ben Lettery, 'the peak of the wet hillside', on the south side above the Clifden road is an isolated summit with commanding views over sea coast and mountain. For a short while in 1919 the seaward view would have included too the Vickers Vimy biplane of Alcock and Brown, tail pointing defiantly upwards, which after the first Atlantic crossing ended with its nose in a bog close by Mannin Bay. The Maam-turks to the east are a zigzag series of beehive-shaped domes with connecting ridges set at angles, very similar to the Twelve Bens but with the conical tops removed. They give a fine ridge walk from Maam Cross to Leenane, which occupied H. C. Hart for 14 hours.

Between the Leenane–Maam road and the Galway–Mayo border is Joyce's Country, named after the family which first settled there-abouts in the thirteenth century. The highest point of this remote mountain area is Bunnacunnen (1,902 feet). Farther east around Cong is one of Ireland's lesser caving areas.

All these mountain groups continue beyond the Mayo border. North of Joyce's Country the Partry Mountains, great areas of grass and peat, reach 2,239 feet at Maumtrasna. These are horizontal beds of Ordovician rocks with precipitous flanks on the north side above the Erriff Valley. Devil's Mother (2,131 feet) rises at the head of Killary Harbour, an arm of the sea ten miles long and half a mile wide, said to be the best example in Ireland of a true fiord—a submerged river valley greatly deepened by ice action. Rain gauges here, at Delphi and Aasleigh, indicate one of the heaviest rainfalls of Ireland. On the shore opposite to Leenane is a group of mountains of gneiss topped by Bengorm (2,303 feet), beyond which the slate and shale Sheefry Mountains, a steep-sided tableland, reach 2,504 feet at Tievummera. To the west beyond Doo Lough are the highest mountains in Connacht, the Mweelrea group; Mweelrea, 'the grey bald mountain top' or 'the smooth mountain flat' (take your pick from the translations), is a magnificent viewpoint at 2,688 feet. There are some steep cliffs above Doo Lough.

The district north of Killary Harbour is called Murrisk; beyond the mountains desolate moorlands continue as far as Clew Bay, broken only by the isolated and shapely quartzite peak, Croagh Patrick (2,510 feet). As long ago as 1796–7, when the Chevalier de la Tocnaye toured Ireland, he was struck by the numbers of pilgrims who went

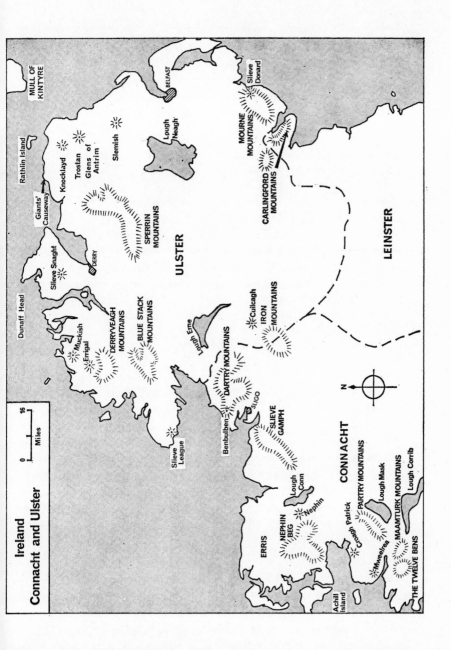

Ireland
Connacht and Ulster

each year to this summit, where St Patrick lived for a time in the fifth century. The numbers impress us equally today when the annual pilgrimage takes place on the last Sunday in July. For example, there were 65,000 of them in 1951, arriving at the top at 120 per minute.

S. de Courcy, a mountaineer among these masses, who started up himself at 5.00 a.m., later described the day:

> . . . Green shoes and red shoes, brown shoes and sandals and sawn off rubber boots, and most wonderful of all, bare feet with shoes stuffed into pockets or slung with knotted laces around the neck filled our company of the heavy nails with due amazement, especially as many of the barefooted pilgrims who at that hour were already descending, must have made the ascent by torchlight or in the dark some hours previously.

> The path up from Murrisk leads southwards past St Patrick's statue to the saddle east of the main peak where the first station or exercise of the pilgrimage is completed. From there, the twelve-hundred-foot-high peak is approached by a dog-leg track leading up across the boulder scree in two reaches to the summit. It may be of interest to record that at 6.30 a.m. seen from the bottom of this path, the ascending and descending streams of people formed, from the skyline at the summit 1,200 feet above, to as far down as the eye could see towards Murrisk 1,300 feet below, a thick unbroken chain of people from three to eight or more abreast. At the summit, in and outside the small concrete and slate oratory of Temple Patrick (Teampall Phadraig, St Patrick's Church) built in 1905 on the site of earlier structures, Mass followed Mass in unbroken sequence from 6.00 a.m. to midday and those who for this purpose had made the ascent, fasting since the previous day, received Holy Communion. On the summit is the second station, as well as the traditional site of St Patrick's bed of which Jocelin says 'and he disposed there five stones and placed himself in the midst'. Around the fringe of the summit is a line of little shelters, built of loose stones and canvas roofs, where tens of thousands of cups of tea are brewed in a fashion rather haphazard but very pleasant to a thirsty pilgrim. The third station, Roilig Mhuire, which completes the pilgrimage exercises, is about 500 feet below the summit on the south-east side . . .

On the north side of Clew Bay is the Curraun Peninsula and off this lies Achill Island, vast peat bog, noted for its tremendous sea-cliffs, especially those at Minaun, Achill Head and below Croaghaun (2,192 feet). The highest point in north Mayo is Nephin (2,646 feet), a quartzite cone over against Lough Conn—the view is extensive because of the isolated position. Westwards is the Nephinbeg range with Slieve Car (2,369 feet); the ridge forks at the southern end, one branch leading by Corrannabinnia to end above Mullarany, the other by Birreencorragh to end above Westport. Around these hills and on northwards is the district known as Erris, a huge barren moorland, the biggest area of peat bog in Ireland. There is so much peat that it does not stop at the shore line but runs on down beyond low water mark. The cliffs between Belmullet and Killala are said to be the finest in the country.

From Lough Conn the Slieve Gamph, actually 'the Stone Mountains', wrongly called 'the Ox Mountains', run north-eastwards across the Sligo border. Dark and heathery, these are an extension of the rocks of Connemara. Beyond Ballysodare Bay is Knocknarea, 'the hill of the executions', with a huge stone cairn 200 feet across, probably an ancient burial place.

East of Sligo is limestone country once again, stretching on across Leitrim and a long salient of Cavan to Fermanagh and Monaghan. The Dartry Hills lie to the north of the Sligo–Manorhamilton road with Truskmore (2,113 feet), 'the big codfish', the highest point showing the usual capping of gritstone on the limestone. The caving prospects hereabouts are undeveloped as yet. Many of the summits are flat-topped plateaux, surrounded by steep rock walls. The western tip of Ben Bulben (1,730 feet), for example, at the end of the range near Sligo juts out like the prow of a ship, while from other aspects it looks the perfect 'table mountain'. Benweeskin and Carrownamaddoo are also striking in outline, the latter a narrow spur more enclosed even than Ben Bulben. This is another botanical paradise. The valleys of Glencar and Glenade, running west and north-west from Manorhamilton, provide spectacular rifts through these hills. A notable feature in both of them are the landslips. When the valleys were ice-filled, the containing walls were scoured out to near vertical; in due course when the ice melted these walls, no longer supported, collapsed in places to produce the land-forms we see today. The so-called 'Swiss Valley' in Glencar is a fine example. South of Glencar are the Castlegal Mountains, the Gaelic name for which is Slieve gan Baiste, 'the mountains without rain'—unique, if true. From Lough Allen the Iron Mountains run across into Ulster. Slieve Anierin (1,927 feet), 'the mountain of iron', is at the western end; Cuilcagh Mountain (2,188 feet) farther east is on the Fermanagh–Cavan border.

*   *   *   *   *

The Province of Ulster incorporates the Six Counties of Northern Ireland—Fermanagh, Tyrone, Derry, Antrim, Down and Armagh, as well as Donegal, Cavan and Monaghan, which form part of the Republic. Monaghan has a large number of little hills but only a few rise above 1,000 feet. In Fermanagh, south and west of Enniskillen, is the most important caving area in Ireland—the usual formation of grits and shales on top of a great limestone plateau riddled with caves and potholes. The hills reach their highest point, 2,188 feet, at Cuilcagh on the Cavan border.

There are three distinct caving districts. The first, on the east side of Cuilcagh, is centred on Swanlibar. Pollnatagha here has a chamber 150 feet by 100 feet. The second on the northern flanks of the same mountain includes the famous Marble Arch Cave, hurriedly visited by Martel in 1895 and since extensively explored and mapped. The Monastir Stream, which sinks on the plateau above, has been traced by fluorescin to Marble Arch, named after a lofty rock bridge which spans the stream near the rising, here called the Cladagh. Several potholes between and parts of the underground course of the river have been entered and followed—the whole adds up to what is perhaps the finest cave system in the British Isles. The third region is farther north centred on Belmore Mountain and Knockmore. Coolarkin Cave, also called Poulnagollum (a favourite cave name), on the north slopes of Belmore, is a large pit with a waterfall and a huge 500-foot passage. Further north beyond Boho are several more caves and potholes. Notable is Noon's Hole, named after an informer who was cast down it to his death in 1826; descended to a depth of 322 feet in 1959, it is the deepest in Ireland. The water emerges at the imposing opening of Ooghboragan, Arch Cave, at the foot of the escarpment; Pollanafrin is another well-known pothole feeding the same outlet.

Donegal, says Hart, has 'some of the highest and finest mountains in Ireland, and the extent of mountainous country is larger than in any other part of Ireland'. Ten of the peaks exceed 2,000 feet and these were traversed in one expedition of under 24 hours in 1961. On the north shores of Donegal Bay the mountains of the Banagh Peninsula rise in parallel lines running north-east to south-west. The highest point is Slieve League (1,972 feet), the south face of which descends precipitously from the summit into the Atlantic Ocean in several miles of impressive sea-cliffs. The seaward face is richly coloured. In the words of Hart:

> This colouring is a remarkable feature. The cliff is well-nigh sheer for 1,000 feet, descending straight from a heathery brink. With the exception of the wonderful cliff seen in Yellowstone Park from 'Inspiration Point', the writer could name no rock face with such an assemblage of hues. Dolerites, diorites, quartzites, schists and conglomerates all help to form this remarkable mountain. Below the Atlantic lights up and enhances the whole scene.

The whole face has been traversed at 700–1,000 feet above sea level, first by Hart who took three days over it, climbing to the top each evening and descending to continue from the same point on the following morning. The cliff-top, too, is not without interest. Between Eagle's Nest (1,750 feet) and the main summit the seaward slopes are extremely steep and those on the landward side fairly so. The resulting crest, only two feet wide in places, is called 'One Man's Path' or 'Pass'; it is easy enough for the level headed but can be avoided, if preferred, by the 'Old Man's Path' some way down the landward side. On the other side of the Banagh Peninsula Slieve Tooey also has precipitous sea-cliffs on its northern slopes.

Inland, north of Donegal Town, are the slate and granite Croaghgorm, or Blue Stack Mountains, where some climbing has been done in recent years above Lough Belshade, 'the lake with the jewel mouth'. Blue Stack itself (2,219 feet) is the highest point, Lavagh More is only a few feet lower. Below these hills the rugged Barnesmore Gap carries the road from Donegal to Derry and south of this a stretch of high heathery moorland leads on to Lough Derg, another famous centre of pilgrimage.

The highest mountain in Donegal is in the north-west—the isolated quartzite cone of Errigal (2,466 feet). Similar in many ways to Croagh Patrick, it needs, however, as Praeger reminds us, 'no association with a saint to make it an object of worship to all lovers of beauty'.

The summit is bifid, with here too a 'One Man's Path', 30 yards long and only two feet wide, connecting the two points. Northwards are the pointed summits of Aghla More and Aghla Beg with Alton Lough, where, Hart tells us, he was once 'solemnly cautioned against swimming on account of the *Phouca*, which lived there and used to mingle with the cattle as a cow and lure one down into the depths. So would he do with mankind . . . Numerous swims in that lake have weakened this prognostication'. Beyond again is Muckish, 'pig's back', a flat-topped hill of mica schist with crags to the north and west. This northern coast is another of fine sea-cliffs, notably at Horn Head.

South and south-east from Errigal summit we look out over the Derryveagh Mountains, 'with bare rock summits looking from above like the wrinkled hide of a petrified elephant', now one of Ireland's great climbing centres, though only developed in the last decade. The Poisoned Glen, immediately below, reminiscent in many ways of Glendalough in Wicklow, is walled by huge granite buttresses which have provided climbs of the highest standards. The Valley probably gets its name from Irish Spurge, a poisonous plant which may once have grown here; it certainly still exists 25 miles away near Lough Swilly. Climbers, who only began hereabouts in 1954, were producing only four years later accounts like this one by Harold Drasdo:

> I placed a peg and roped across the slabs, protected from the rappel point, until, laybacking from the rope against a vertical kerb, I could reach a thin fissure, secure piton and stirrup and stand up; then, with two or three pegs, a foothold a little higher. A short rest, pressed against the clean cold stone down which at this point water was trickling: time to feel the damp neuter breath of the granite close to one's face. Movements became complicated. The climbing rope was locking. I descended to the first peg, settled into the stirrups, recovered the rappel rope, belayed Nev . . . He moved up to the rappel point, unclipped the climbing rope, returned to his stance. Rope-drag relieved a moment, I stripped the crack, placed a second rappel peg, made a second rappel and, laybacking against another vertical facet, established myself in stirrups from a tiny rock spike, strange aberration in the naked slabs.

We find here, as elsewhere in the country, the spectacle of all stages of climbing development from the primitive to the modern taking place simultaneously.

22 *Ben Bulben, Co. Sl*

At the head of the Poisoned Glen the Ballaghgeeha Gap, 'the windy pass', leads over to Glen Veagh, which runs in the usual south-west to north-east direction. There are climbing crags in both directions —above Lough Veagh on the one hand and above Lough Barra, on the slopes of Slieve Snaght (2,240 feet), on the other. Here there are climbs of all standards on granite crags, easily accessible from the road and rapidly increasing in importance.

On the Inishowen Peninsula between Lough Foyle and Lough Swilly the last group of Donegal mountains reaches 2,019 feet at another Slieve Snaght. There are more sea-cliffs here, notably the 700-foot Dunaff Head, commanding a remarkable view towards Scotland which includes the Paps of Jura and Arran. The distance, incidentally, of the visible horizon for an observer at a known height above sea level can in fact be easily calculated. At these latitudes and taking into account atmospheric refraction the approximate formula is $H = \frac{1}{2}d^2$, where H is the height of the observer in feet and d the distance of the visible horizon in miles. To decide whether two mountains are visible from one another across the sea, we work out the distance of the visible horizon for each. If the two distances added together are less than the actual distance separating the summits, then one mountain cannot be seen from the other. In this case the Paps of Jura (2,571 feet) give d of 72 miles, while the corresponding figures for Dunaff Head are 700 feet and 35 miles, so that they would be just inter-visible if 107 miles apart. In fact the line of sight is only 85 miles and there can be no doubt about it. Conditions of exceptional refraction which occasionally occur may sometimes account for reported sightings in places where calculation has in fact indicated that this is impossible.

The Sperrin Mountains, gneiss and schists with a heavy covering of peat, separate Derry from Tyrone; Sawel (2,240 feet), the highest point, is actually on the county boundary. Northwards, outliers of the Antrim basalt reach to over 1,000 feet in Derry, while southwards in Tyrone there are numerous hills up to 1,800 feet.

The north-east corner of Ireland, separated from Scotland's Mull of Kintyre by a strait only 13 miles wide, is County Antrim. The scenery is dominated by the largest lava plateau in the British Isles, basalts which welled up through cracks in the lower rocks and spread out to cover some 1,600 square miles. The centre later collapsed forming the basin now occupied by Lough Neagh. The hexagonal columns, outstanding feature of the renowned Giant's Causeway and of other local headlands, were formed when the lava cooled; notable, too, are the steep black walls of lava which overlook the Glens of Antrim nearby. The county summit, Trostan (1,817 feet), is in the north among these glens, of which Glenariff is the finest.

Beneath the lavas are rock strata, such as chalk, characteristic of southern England. The juxtaposition of black and white rocks is particularly marked on Rathlin Island, which Charles Kingsley in *Westward Ho!* likened to a drowned magpie. The island was the scene of Robert Bruce's encounter with the inspirational spider. The same rock contrast is shown in Knocklayd above Ballycastle, where basalt stands above chalk which stands in turn on schists. An elaborate hoax took place here in 1788 when a minor bog slide near the summit was reported in newspapers as a volcanic eruption—'Our fears were very much increased in the evening by a most uncommon noise from Knocklade, the top of which burst, and the discharge of burning matter and hot stones from it was truly alarming, killing several cattle in the adjacent fields, many cabins were thrown down, and several people are missing . . . supposed to have been overtaken by the burning matter, which was thirty perches in breadth, and ran near a mile and a half.' Later accounts were even more lurid—one describing the destruction of a village, another an inspection of the smoking crater 100 yards in diameter. It was undoubtedly a gigantic leg-pull, arising, it has been suggested, out of the controversy then current in geological circles between 'Neptunists' and 'Vulcanists'. Only a mile or two away at Kinbane the chalk stands for a change on top of the basalt.

All the coast scenery in fact is very fine and overshadows that of the mountains. It is not mountaineers' country like Donegal or Kerry, but, as Hart quaintly puts it:

. . . is more highly cultivated and more civilised than a climber with a proper sense of his calling could possibly approve of. It suggests driving, bicycling, picnics, good dinners, and evening dress more than knickers and hard work.

On southwards the hills get lower, but in passing we must notice Slemish Mountain near Ballymena—another associated with St Patrick, for here he spent six youthful years in captivity as a swineherd. The hills continue almost into the suburbs of Belfast; Cave Hill has caves and a little rock climbing, then farther round are Divis and Black Hill, now carrying television masts, the latest symbols of modernity.

The Mourne Mountains, perhaps the best-known Irish hill group, sweep down to the sea, as every schoolchild knows, in the extreme south of County Down between Newcastle and Rostrevor; from their summits we look across Carlingford Lough to the hills of Leinster. The Kilkeel to Hilltown road, the Spelga Pass, divides them into two, leaving most of the major hills in the eastern block, often called the Mourne Trident. The prongs of the trident are three lines of hills running south-east from Slieve Commedagh, 'the mountain of watching'. The eastern prong includes Slieve Donard (2,796 feet), the highest point both of these hills and of Ulster, named after Saint Domhanghort. The central prong ends in Slieve Binnian, a long rocky ridge which R. L. Praeger describes as 'the back of a two-mile Diplodocus'. The third of these ridge lines, above the Spelga Pass, includes the rocky Slieve Bearnagh. The prongs enclose two deep valleys, the Annalong Valley to the east, and the Silent Valley, once called Happy Valley, now the site of two dams and extensive Belfast Waterworks. The initial scheme was completed in 1932; after World War II a tunnel through Slieve Binnian diverted water from the Annalong into the Silent Valley and the storage capacity of the latter was increased by the construction of a second dam. The Water Commissioners' catchment area is delineated by a boundary wall, which passes along the two outer prongs. To follow the wall from end to end gives a fine marathon walk. Beyond the Spelga Pass is a collection of bird names—Hen, Cock, Pigeon and Eagle Mountains; on the last two are some of the highest crags in the Mournes.

The rock is granite, contemporary with the Antrim basalt and much newer than the granites of Wicklow or Armagh. Some of the rock exposures are hill-top tors and pinnacles, such as for example the Castles of Commedagh, described as 'piled pancakes', and the Binnian Tors. There are higher crags also. The weathering is such that much of it is difficult or impossible to climb except by the most straightforward lines. A resemblance to the Isle of Arran has been noted and this other area of granite mountains is indeed not far away across the water.

*   *   *   *   *

The climber on Slieve Donard's summit can see on a clear day the mountains of Donegal and Wicklow, as well as those of Arran and South Scotland, Cumberland and North Wales, while nearer at hand floating in mid sea is the Isle of Man, the hills of which reach just over 2,000 feet at Snaefell. There is a railway to the summit from Laxey. Several other hills exceed 1,000 feet but there is little exposure of rock; almost all Manx climbing is on sea-cliffs.

EIGHT

Scotland—General
and Southern

Scotland is by far the most mountainous of the countries of the British Isles. While England, Wales and Ireland have less than 30 3,000-foot mountains between them, Scotland has no less than 543 called, as we have seen, Munros. Twelve of these exceed 4,000 feet in height and Ben Nevis, the highest point in Britain, lies only 1,000 feet below the permanent snowline at this latitude.

For convenience of description we can divide the country into five regions. The first of these, the Southern Uplands, lies south of a line joining the Firths of Forth and Clyde. Between here and a line joining Stonehaven and Helensburgh are the Central Lowlands where the majority of the people live. North of this lie the Highlands, divided into two by the Great Glen running from Fort William to Inverness. South of the Great Glen, in what are broadly termed the Grampian Mountains, are all the highest summits; north of it are the more lonely, wilder Northern and Western Highlands with many fine peaks of striking form in a variety of rock types. The fifth area embraces the Scottish Islands from Arran in the Clyde through the Inner and Outer Hebrides to Orkney and Shetland in the far north.

Of the four major forces for mountain preservation which we noted south of the Border, three are active in Scotland, but as yet there are no National Parks. The principal National Forest Parks are Argyll (100 sq. miles), Glen Trool in Galloway (200 sq. miles), Glen More in the Cairngorms (20 sq. miles) and the Queen Elizabeth in the Trossachs (60 sq. miles), while the 250 sq. miles of the Border Forest Park are shared between Roxburghshire and Northumberland. The Nature Conservancy holds Ben Lawers, Perthshire, and Beinn Eighe, Ross-shire, as well as St Kilda, the 40 sq. miles of Rum and more than 30 sq. miles in the Cairngorms, while the National Trust for Scotland owns mountain areas in Kintail and Glencoe and on Arran.

In 1961 an interesting survey of the Highlands was carried out by W. H. Murray, a noted Scottish climber, on behalf of the National Trust for Scotland. Asked to delineate and report on all areas of outstanding natural beauty, he chose eventually 21 as follows:

Moidart; Glen Nevis; Loch Arkaig; Knoydart; Glenelg; Kintail; Applecross; Ben Damph and Coulin Forests; Torridon; Loch Maree; Strathnasheallag and Fisherfield Forests; Inverpolly and Glencanisp Forests; Glen Affric; The Cairngorms; Balmoral Forest; Tummel Valley; Benalder Range; Blackmount, Rannoch and Glencoe; Glen Lyon; Loch Lomond; The Trossachs.

He draws attention in his report to the great changes wrought in recent years by the Hydro-Electric Board and by the Forestry Commission (now the greatest landowner in Scotland)—their activities destroying substantially the scenic amenities of one area, (Glen Garry, Glen Strathfarrer and Glen Cannich, for example, have suffered serious disfigurement), in another leaving the scenery relatively untouched. He deplores the spread of motor roads, which are replacing some of the fine cross-country paths in mountain areas, leading as he says 'to an absurd situation in which the tourist can travel by car even farther, yet finds that his new roads take him through country less worth seeing than before'. It is worthwhile quoting his conclusion in full, for these remarks apply with equal force to all our mountains:

Without further multiplying instances, it can now be seen that the changing face of Scotland has suffered in the past haphazard change, and that many more changes, from many different quarters, threaten it in the immediate future. The ugliness that has grown up in so many of our towns arrived there insidiously, creeping in by degrees through lack of overall direction, foresight or control. The same situation is arising in the Scottish Highlands. The outstanding beauty of the Highland scene, which is one of the nation's greatest assets, has been haphazardly expended and no account kept. The wasting away of this asset is bound to continue and to accelerate unless discrimination and control are brought to bear by some body created for the purpose and granted powers by government, so that checks and safeguards may be instituted. If action to that good end be not

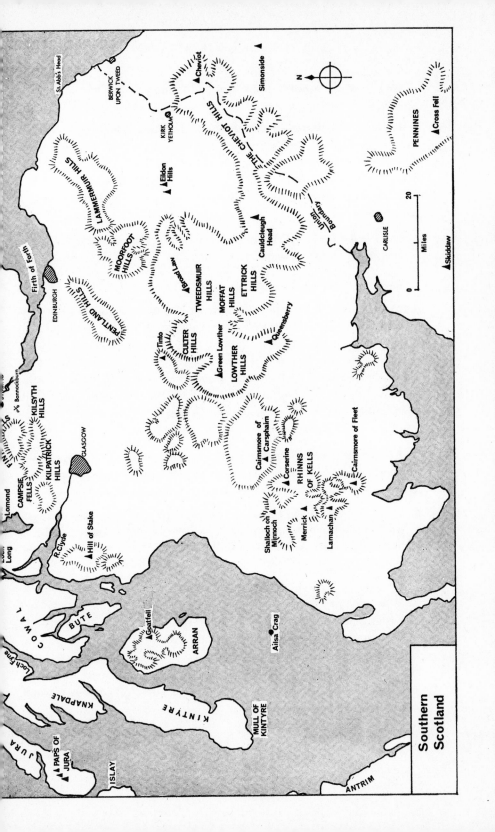

Southern Scotland

taken now, the Scottish people will lose by neglect what remains of their natural heritage.

From the earliest times local people and huntsmen may well have crossed the passes, and even the summits, of the Scottish mountains but until the eighteenth century travellers from a distance found them largely inaccessible due to lack of roads and facilities. John Taylor, who climbed Mount Keene on his way from Glen Esk to Glen Dee in 1618, wrote of it:

> Up and downe, I thinke this hill is six miles, the way so uneven, stony, and full of bogges, quagmires, and long heath, that a dogge with three legs will out-runne a horse with foure; for doe what wee could wee were foure hours before we could passe it.

Defoe, who was here at the same time on his famous tour, described his journey, as one writer has said, 'in terms such as might now be used of Matabeleland or the Pamirs'. Military roads were made before and after '45, but the present road system mostly dates back to about 1800. After the disaster at Culloden the wanderings of Bonnie Prince Charlie provided a saga of mountain travel, yet he and his companions could have had no eye for the scenery except as a cover from their ruthless hunters. And, as all heroes should, he got away!

A few years later Thomas Pennant, whom we have met south of the Border, came twice to Scotland and then wrote a book about it. He climbed a few hills including Beinn na Caillich in Skye, finding:

> . . . the top flat and naked, with an artificial cairn of a most enormous size, reported to have been the place and sepulchre of a gigantic woman in the days of Fingal. The prospect to the west was that of desolation itself— a savage series of rude mountains, discoloured, black and red, as by the rage of fire . . .

When in 1773 Boswell and Johnson made their tour of Scotland and the Isles, they found the people interesting but the mountains dull:

'The appearance is that of matter incapable of form or usefulness, dismissed by Nature from her care, and disinherited of her favours, left in its original elemental state, or quickened only with one sullen power of useless vegetation.' Yet both left copious accounts of their adventures.

24 *Ben Nevis from Corp*
25 (Overleaf) *The Moffat H*

Dr John MacCulloch, whose four-volume work on the Highlands and Western Isles appeared in 1824, was probably the first genuine 'fell walker' to appear on the scene. He claimed to 'have ascended almost every principal mountain in Scotland', an extravagant claim perhaps, but he certainly had an impressive list. His interest was geology—'divine maid, who urged him to risk his neck, every day on mountain and precipice'. Another prominent mountain climber in the same period was Rev. Thomas Grierson from Kirkcudbrightshire.

James Forbes, scientist and pioneer mountaineer in Scotland and Norway, explored many parts of the country in the 1830s and 1840s. He made the first ascent of Sgurr nan Gillean in Skye and cut the first mountaineer's step in the snows of Ben Nevis:

> We kept on the rock as long as we could, and at length found that there only intervened between us and the ridge a short, steep ascent of drifted snow, most truly Alpine. It was too late to think of receding, and it was not very far; so assuming my new mahogany tripod as an Alpine stock, I proceeded foremost to make steps in the most approved Swiss fashion . . . The upper few yards were so steep that I actually could not get one foot stuck into the snow before the other, and had to get along sideways.

During the next few decades the sporting potentialities of these mountains were gradually developed. Though large areas were set aside for stalking there was free access for the relatively small number of climbers and walkers who came out of season. In 1859 Charles Weld, a member of the Alpine Club, described the Cuillin Hills of Skye in these words—'Peaks and pinnacles, jagged crests and fantastic outlines; a wilderness of weird shapes, dark, solemn and awful' and drew the attention of the Club to one pinnacle in particular, said on the Admiralty Chart to be inaccessible. This was not climbed until 1880 but in the meantime we increasingly find the famous names from the world of climbing among the hills of the north; Skye in particular with its attractive mountains, unmatched anywhere in these islands, was a Mecca for strong parties. Scottish alpinists, such as Prof. G. Ramsay and W. W. Naismith, took a hand too, so that the formation of some sort of mountaineering club became inevitable. Two were in fact founded within a very short period—first, the Cairngorm Club, which has remained to this day a purely local club based on the north-east coast, and second, the Scottish Mountaineering Club, now the senior national organization.

In these early days winter climbing in Scotland was regarded mainly as training for mountaineering in the great ranges of the world and, apart from a few great ridges like those of Ben Nevis, most of the sport was found on ice or hard snow in gullies. The outstanding climber of the years up to 1914 was Harold Raeburn and here we see him typically in action on the face of Ben Nevis:

> Round the top of the gully—rather shallow scoop now—up which we were cutting, stretched the threatening line of the summit cornice. This did not look very high from farther down, but on approach was seen to rear its breaker-like crest, more than two-man height above the slope. Obviously our only chance here was to traverse out to our right where a rib of ice-covered rock ran up to meet the cornice, reducing it to half the height, and where it was only slightly overhanging. This way eventually 'went', but the 'Comb' was game to the last, and I must confess to a feeling of helplessness for a moment as I stood on my ice-axe, driven horizontally into the vertical snow wall, some hundreds of feet of little less than vertical ice-plastered rocks stretching away down into the depths of the mist beneath, while my fingers slid helplessly from the glassy surface of the cornice névé, in the vain endeavour to find or make a hold by which I might haul myself up. The problem was solved by a retreat, until Phildius was able to pass me up his axe. Then the ice-plating was quickly shattered, and with fingers well crooked in the tough névé, a steady drag landed the body over the cornice lip, and Phildius soon followed.

He goes on to compare the difficulties of the climb ($5\frac{1}{2}$ hours for 450 feet) with those of the Z'mutt Arête of the Matterhorn, where 4,000 feet had taken him only 11 hours; 'in everything but vertical height the Nevis climb was the more difficult and sporting'.

It was not until the 1930s that changes in outlook began to appear. The range of attack, formerly limited, was widely extended and all types of climb—buttresses, ridges and faces—came to be tackled under various sorts of winter conditions. Here are W. H. Murray and W. M. Mackenzie, leaders of this phase, on a typical route of the period. With A. M. MacAlpine they have started the Observatory Ridge Climb on Ben Nevis at 9 a.m. on a winter's day, now close on nightfall and high up on the climb they find so much powder snow on the rocks that they are forced to traverse into a gully alongside:

. . . the steps had to be well made, not too far apart. This meant heavy labour; digging, excavating, cutting, and at last climbing, until one's arms and shoulders ached with the incessant work, whilst one's mind kept alert to the faultless control of body movement. We grew more and more tired, and realizing it, more and more determined. It was beyond the power of one man to lead throughout, so each of us took turns at going first, flogging out the upward passage, until his weariness resulted in too slow progress, when he would retire in favour of the next man.

In two hours we reached the first ice-wall. Until my days are ended I shall never forget that situation. Crouching below the pitch amidst showers of ice-chips, I fed out the frozen rope while Mackenzie hewed mightily at the ice above, his torch weirdly bobbing up and down in the dark and the ice brilliantly sparkling under its beam. Looking down, I could see just a short curve of grey snow plunging into the lower darkness, then nothing until the twinkling lights of the Spean Valley, four thousand feet below.

Murray's brilliant descriptive writing did much to inspire the recent generations of Scottish climbers in the truly remarkable expansion which has taken place since World War II. 'The present-day formula', writes an expert, 'is that any summer rock climb (provided it is suitably plastered in snow) makes a good winter climb'; this even applies to routes of the highest summer standard which might be expected to be impossible in adverse conditions. Fine winter climbs have been done also on crags which, because of vegetation or poor-quality rock, are unsuitable for summer climbing. The popular districts for winter mountaineering are Glencoe, the Cairngorms and Lochnagar, Creag Meaghaidh and Ben Nevis. The last was notable as the scene of a *tour de force* in 1959 when the ascent of the oddly-named Point Five Gully occupied a party of four for five days. Large numbers of pitons were used; each evening they returned by abseil (controlled descent of the rope), spent the night at the climbers' hut below the face, then climbed back with the aid of the ropes on the following morning to begin where they had left off. As Ian Clough tells it:

. . . I climbed towards the place where we had left in the rock-pegs last year. Then I saw a peg with a piece of nylon hanging from it in the groove on the left of the ice bulge, just above where our pegs should have been. Reaching it, I clipped in and then saw another peg under the ice on the right. Soon I was standing on an étrier hanging from this peg and knocking in a further rock-peg on the same traversing line. Next I used an étrier hanging from an ice-peg and, with another ice-peg for a hand-hold, I was over the crux. Another 25 feet up I found a place for a stance, but it took another 1½ hours before I had found places for satisfactory rock-peg belays. With the rope fastened to the pegs, I roped off. Another day's work was at end.

Dr Tom Patey sums up modern Scottish winter mountaineering thus:
'Its principles are founded on the best traditions of British Mountaineering, and it teaches virtues which are the essence of successful Alpine and Himalayan climbing—speed, resourcefulness and, above all, accurate route finding. Nevertheless I would recoil from describing Scottish winter climbing merely in terms of training for (so-called) Greater Mountaineering. That would be heresy; the Scottish brand of winter mountaineering is unique!'

For most of its history the development of summer climbing in Scotland has tended to parallel, though rather later in time, that of the Lake District and North Wales. We can detect also on the literary side a similar parallel progress. A. E. Maylard, writing in 1899, could point to substantial changes after only a single decade:

... the crisp morning air filled with the music of bird voices ... produced in one that indescribable feeling of enthusiasm with which one starts for a mountain expedition in the Highlands.

Having given way in this short period to the full 'blood and thunder' narrative of the early climbers:

Grasping some excellent hand-holds, and resting his feet on some sloping slabs underneath an overhanging ledge, the leader pulled himself up a foot or two, and hanging by one arm, back downwards, fumbled about for hand-holds higher up, and strove to get foot or knee into the narrow vertical crack ...

In the ensuing years, as the sport developed its own methods and traditions, descriptions became more clinical and less uninhibited. Progress was slow. The piton and associated climbing tactics, putting in a surreptitious appearance in the 1930s, gradually won acceptance. Here is Dr J. H. B. Bell on Lochnagar in 1941:

. . . The leader here discarded boots. On the right was an edge above a vertical wall. It was necessary to lean across this and drive a piton into a crack in the wall. A stone was used for this purpose. Even in stockings the balance was most delicate and the friction doubtful. The problem is to stand on the piton and reach up to a rounded flat ledge in order to swarm up on to it. There is a good pulling-edge beyond, but it is a very severe pitch. One is not yet out of the wood, as there is over 20 feet of very difficult climbing, somewhat complicated with blueberry and crowberry plants, before one reaches an upper terrace with a good belay.

Post-war developments in Scottish rock climbing have been extensive and far reaching. Large numbers of Scotsmen climb and standards are as high here as anywhere in these Islands. Glencoe has received particularly detailed attention, providing this sort of work for the expert, here described by Robin Campbell:

> Two monstrous overhangs with a lesser one in between about sums it up. You go swinging across the lesser one in slings or étriers, from peg to spike to peg to spike to peg, then make a last big reach to a last big spike and after that it's only desperate to a belay right out on the edge of everything.

What was, perhaps, the earliest use of skis in Scotland was described by W. W. Naismith in 1892:

> For the sake of any uninitiated, it may be explained that skis (pron.'shes') are wooden snow skates, 7 feet long and 3 to 4 inches wide, largely used throughout the northern parts of Europe and Asia . . . On 12th March, shortly after a considerable fall of snow, M. T. G. and W. W. N. climbed the Campsies behind Milton and followed the crest of the ridge for two miles to the Meikle Bin . . . The skis were not of much use when ascending but upon level ground, and especially where the snow was soft, better progress was made with their aid than without them, while a very slight gradient was sufficient to get up tremendous speed during the descent. When the angle was too steep to risk, the skis were slipped off and turned into an improvised toboggan . . . Of course the party came to grief several times, but they returned home well pleased with their experiment.

'In the Alps', he goes on to say, 'it is not unlikely that the sport may eventually become popular.'

Ski-ing by mountaineers, which developed only slowly, was devoted mainly to this type of cross-country travel. The Scottish Ski Club founded in 1907 hardly survived the War, but in 1929 it was revived with more of an Alpine, or downhill only, outlook. A hut was opened on Ben Lawers in 1937 and the sport was actively pursued both here and in the Cairngorms by a membership which reached over 400 just before World War II.

The last decade has seen a very great increase in interest and a determined effort to turn Scotland into a winter sports country. Hotels, ski schools with Continental instructors, access roads, chair-lifts and ski tows have sprung up in the four main areas, which are: Strathspey and Badenoch north of the Cairngorms, Deeside on the south side of the Cairngorms, Glenshee farther south still and Glencoe in the west. Now further huge sums are to be spent to extend these facilities and to provide ice rinks, swimming pools, dance halls and so on to cater for bad weather in the day time and après-ski entertainment. Meanwhile Ben Lawers and Ben Wyvis remain for those who do not like the crowds. In fact, as things stand at present, organization is confined to a limited area and there is still plenty of scope for the langlauf type of skier.

We note briefly in passing the rather specialized preservation of Scotland's mountains for the sports of stalking and shooting. Of the country's 30,000 square miles around 4,000 square miles have been set aside as deer forests. It has been argued that, but for this state of affairs, the red deer would by now have been exterminated as a pest, yet it would be equally possible to preserve the species by a method which did not involve shutting off such large areas of recreational countryside. The hills were given over to deer, however, long before the walker and climber appeared on the scene and every effort has always been made to avoid conflict between the devotees of these various sports. What is a sport? It is not appropriate to discuss here the ethics of killing, but some attitudes are certainly peculiar. 'To those of us who hunt', wrote Fairfax-Blakeborough 25 years ago, 'sport connotes some open air diversion in which man is assisted by dumb animals.' He dismissed walking, climbing and caving as mere pastimes; hunting, on the other hand, where the only possible assistance by the dumb animal would seem to involve not running away too rapidly, is sport!

* * * * *

We begin our review of the mountains of Scotland near the English border, across which for most of its length the hills roll without interruption. Here are the Southern Uplands divided by Nithsdale into two distinct scenic areas. Eastwards almost to the coast are rounded, vegetation-covered hills of uniform height with occasional isolated hill groups of volcanic origin very similar to those in adjacent Northumberland. On the other side of Nithsdale large granite masses produce wilder and more rugged scenery in the district known as Galloway. The 2,000-foot hills, totalling 148, were tabulated some years ago by P. Donald in the *Scottish Mountaineering Club Journal*, though no one as yet calls them 'Donalds'.

Galloway is noted for many curiously-named hills; some, like Millyea from Meall Liath, 'grey hill', and Milldown from Meall Donn, 'brown hill', are of Gaelic origin, corrupted by folks who no longer understand the meaning; others, like Curleywee, Windy Standard, Irongallows, Minoch on Shalloch, seem outstandingly imaginative. There are five principal hill groups. East of Newton Stewart the Cairnsmore of Fleet group reaches 2,331 feet; northwards beyond the New Galloway road the second of these blocks, which includes Lamachan (2,349 feet) and Curleywee, is bounded in the north by the beautiful Glen Trool, scene of a battle in Robert Bruce's time. This is now part of the Glen Trool Forest Park, as is Merrick (2,764 feet) the culminating point of the range running on northwards. This, the highest point in south Scotland, bears its share of interesting names—a narrow ridge on its north, called the Spear, separating deep corries called Fang of Merrick and How of Cauldron. Parallel and eastwards beyond a moorland basin is the Rhinns of Kells, which reach 2,688 feet at Corserine, while on north-eastwards the fifth group has its highest point in Cairnsmore of Carsphairn (2,612 feet). During recent years a little rock climbing has been done on isolated crags in these hills, but it is predominantly walking country, wild, remote and little visited, though eaten into extensively by those twin menaces—the Hydro-Electric Board and the Forestry Commission.

Between Nithsdale and the upper valleys of the Annan and the Clyde are the Lowther, or Lead Hills (Green Lowther, 2,403 feet). These are smooth and green and there is no rock climbing. Leadhills Village, formerly centre of the local lead mining, claims to be the highest in Scotland. A long ridge extends south-eastwards from the group to Queensbury while far to the north above upper Clydesdale stands the isolated Tinto, a volcanic laccolite and a fine viewpoint with a summit indicator. The main line railway to Glasgow crosses from Annandale to Clydesdale by Beattock summit beyond which, stretching to the upper Tweed Valley are the Culter Hills, which include Culter Fell (2,454 feet) and the quaintly-named Gathersnow Hill. Eastwards now, between here and the upper Yarrow Valley, lie the extensive Tweedsmuir, or Manor Hills (Broad Law, 2,754 feet), while contiguous to the south in the angle between Annandale and Moffat Water are the Moffat Hills (White Coomb, 2,695 feet). There are climbing possibilities here. South-east of the line of Moffat Water and the upper Yarrow are the Ettrick Hills culminating in Ettrick Pen.

The watershed of the country runs almost due east now over Cauldcleuch Head (2,028 feet) to join the Cheviot and the English border. The main summits of the Cheviot are in England, though Windygyle and Auchope Cairn are shared; the highest point on the Union Boundary is on the south-west ridge of Cheviot.

Also in Roxburghshire, close to Melrose, are the isolated Eildon Hills, only 1,385 feet but outstanding as the remains of old groups of volcanoes.

We now move northwards across the plain of the lower Tweed to the hills which line the southern side of the Firth of Forth. The east coast railway to Edinburgh bypasses these at the seaward end. On the border between Berwick and East Lothian are the Lammermuirs, a 30-mile tract of bare moorland of gentle outline with several hill-top forts. The highest point is Meikle Says Law (1,749 feet) towards the west. There is fine cliff scenery around St Abb's Head where the range reaches the sea. The grassy Moorfoot Hills, only 15 miles south of Edinburgh, comprise three parallel hill groups separated by the lines South Esk–Craighope–Leithen Water and Dewar Burn–Glentress Water. The highest points of these are Windlestraw Law (2,161 feet) in the eastern, Blackhope Scar (2,136 feet) in the central and Dundreich (2,040 feet) in the western. This is popular ski country. Farther west the Pentland Hills, rising almost in the suburbs of Edinburgh, run south-westwards for 15 miles towards Peebles. There is a little rock climbing on Caerketton, the hill nearest the City, and indeed on Salisbury Crags within the City boundary. The nearby summit of Allermuir is said to command a view stretching from the Cheviot to the Cairngorms. Of Carnethy (1,890 feet) farther on, Sir Walter Scott wrote: 'I never saw anything more beautiful than the ridge of Carnethy against a clear frosty sky . . . The hills glowed like purple amethysts . . . I never saw a finer screen than Pentland, considering that it is neither rocky or highly elevated.' Scald Law only eight feet higher is the summit of the range.

A series of hills of volcanic origin run across the Midland Plain of Scotland in a north-easterly direction from the Firth of Clyde to the east coast in Angus. These, known collectively as the Lennox Hills, are of special importance because of their proximity to the most thickly populated parts of the country, so that their influence is out of proportion with their mere size. All give outstandingly fine views of the Highlands across the north part of the Plain. The hills of north-west Renfrewshire reach 1,711 feet at Hill of Stake and there is a little climbing thereabouts. Beyond the Clyde the Kilpatrick Hills above Dumbarton have two equal highest points, Fynloch Hill and Duncomb, both 1,313 feet, while the crag of the Whangie here provides the nearest rock climbing to Glasgow. The flat-topped Campsie Fells (Earl's Seat, 1,894 feet) rising beyond Strathblane are steep and rocky on their southern faces, which coincide with one of the great fault lines. There is climbing above Blanefield, while nearby are the famous Ballagan Beds, where over 200 distinct strata have been laid bare in an amphitheatre cut by the Ballagan Burn. The Kilsyth Hills (Meikle Bin, 1,870 feet) continue the line eastwards, while to the north towards Stirling are the Fintry Hills. Stirling Castle commands the gap between here and the Ochil Hills, through which flows the River Forth. Nearby Edward II fought the disastrous Bannockburn. The 24-mile range of the Ochil Hills (Ben Cleuch, 2,363 feet) continues the hill line north-eastwards. The craggy peak of Dumyat at the western end has a few climbs, otherwise most of this is walkers' territory with the usual fine views of the Highlands. Eastwards in Fife the Lomond Hills (West Lomond, 1,713 feet) are of interest geologically and botanically and there is a little rock climbing. The Sidlaw Hills (Craigowe, 1,493 feet) extend the main ridge line beyond the Tay Valley, with Perth commanding the gap. These hills run on almost to Montrose separating the fertile plains of Strathmore from the Carse of Gowrie. Prominent all along here in the northward view rise rank upon rank of higher, wilder mountains—the Grampians.

NINE

The Grampian Mountains

The mountains of Perthshire form the frontier of the Highlands facing out across the hills and plains of the Central Lowlands. The line roughly from Helensburgh to Stonehaven, which demarcates the Highlands, is completed by the Ben Lomond group in Stirlingshire and the southern Cairngorms in Angus. There are four of Murray's 'regions of outstanding beauty' here, namely, the Tummel Valley, Glen Lyon, The Trossachs and Loch Lomond.

Loch Lomond, over 20 miles long and comparatively close to the more populated parts of the country, was described as long ago as 1658 as 'small mediterrane surrounded with woods, mountains, rocky, boggy, sandy, and mirey earth'. The ascent of Ben Lomond (3,192 feet), which towers above the lake has always been popular, travellers finding difficulties according to their abilities and imaginations. MacCulloch, for example, thought it easy, not so Mary Howitt (1822):

> We found the ascent from Rowardennan a laborious task of four hours. We waded deep in heather, crossed rocky and impetuous torrents, laboured up acclivities only to see unsuspected hollows which must be descended. The bogs which intercepted our course every few yards required a good deal of boldness, contrivance, and circumspection to pass.

A winter ascent was made in 1812 by a party which was 'obliged to take knives and to cut foot-steps in the frozen snow' to get up. A significant event this in the history of home mountaineering, and indeed in that of world mountaineering.

The Trossachs, 'the Bristly Country', is the name given to an area centred on Loch Katrine and bounded by Lochs Voil, Lubnaig, Chon and Ard. Ben Ledi (2,873 feet) above Callander, with a view from Nevis to Tinto and the Cairngorms to Arran, is the highest point. The double-peaked Ben Venue (2,393 feet) by the foot of Loch Katrine, the setting of Sir Walter Scott's 'Lady of the Lake', is also very worthy. Many of the early visitors who impressed even MacCulloch by their numbers were inspired by this poem. The Trossachs with its mixture of lake, wooded hillside and rugged mountain, the classical scenery of the Scottish Highlands, is still much loved by tourists.

Between Loch Voil and Glen Dochart is a group of high mountains which includes the shapely schistose masses of Ben More (3,843 feet), a huge sugar loaf and one of the most majestic and prominent mountains in Scotland, Stobinian, a perfect cone of 3,827 feet, and several others above 3,000 feet. Ben More was climbed in 1769 by astronomers to observe a transit of Venus. In describing a walk here in May, 1892, W. W. Naismith first enunciated his 'Rule' for calculating times for easy mountain expeditions—'an hour for every three miles on the map, with an additional hour for every 2,000 feet of ascent'. This is still often quoted, though curiously the years have changed it to only 1,500 feet of ascent per hour. They must have been tougher in the old days after all.

West of the Ben More group on the far side of Glen Falloch is an extensive range of mica-schist mountains, which culminates in Ben Lui (Beinn Laoigh, 3,708 feet). The very steep north-eastern corrie gives some useful snow climbing, the Central Gully in particular is a classic climb.

It is convenient to divide the remainder of the Perthshire mountains into five groups divided by the valleys of the Tay and its various tributaries. The most southerly of these, Strathearn, is bounded on the south by a compact group of mountains which includes Stuc a' Chroin and Ben Vorlich (3,224 feet), where MacCulloch found 'a continued succession of bold precipices and deep hollows, of ravines and torrents, and of woods dispersed in every mode of picturesque distribution'. This same energetic traveller also climbed Ben Chonzie, the only 3,000-foot summit in the extensive tract of high moorland separating Strathearn from Strathtay.

Between Strathtay and Glen Lyon is a further conglomeration of little-known hills, with one hill—Ben Lawers—that is very well known.

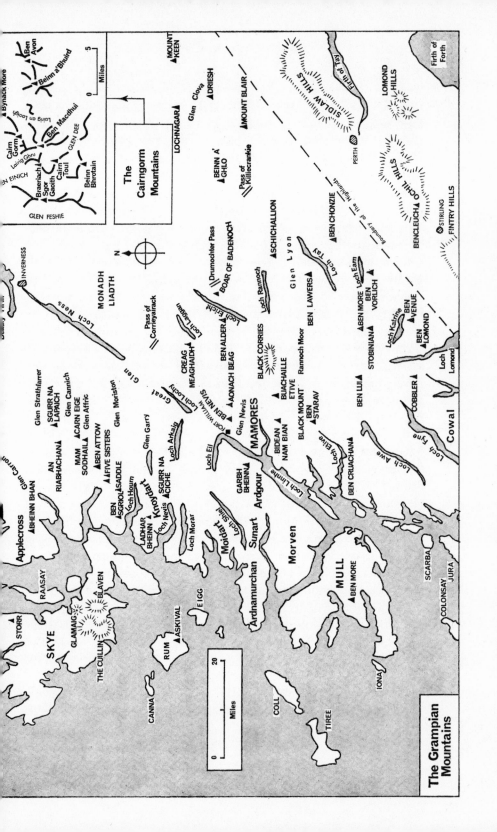

The Grampian Mountains

Between Glen Dochart and Glen Lochay the highest point is Meall Glas, while round the head-waters of the Lochay is the Forest of Mamlorn, which reaches 3,530 feet at Beinn Heasgarnich. All this is potential ski country, though rather remote. Farther to the east close to the head of Loch Tay are Meall Ghaordie and Meall nan Tarmachan, the highest points respectively of the western and eastern groups of the so-called Killin Hills. Ben Lawers (3,984 feet), the highest mountain in Perthshire, rises from the northern shores of Loch Tay. This mica schist peak, culminating point once again of a host of satellite summits, has several claims to distinction. A large portion of it belongs to the National Trust for Scotland. It is renowned for the wealth of its plant life, due, say the naturalists, to the fact that the summit escaped the last glaciation. MacCulloch thought it noteworthy that 'the ascent is so easy as to permit riding to the summit'. A party of Royal Engineers camped on the top for several months in 1852, while the triangulation of the United Kingdom was in progress. In 1878 a patriotic local man arranged for a summit cairn to be built raising the height to 4,000 feet, but this unfortunately did not survive for more than 20 years. Nowadays this district is one of Scotland's most important ski centres and the Scottish Ski Club has a hut in Coire Odhar on Beinn Ghlas.

Glen Lyon, around 35 to 40 miles long, has been described as the longest glen in Scotland; it 'exemplifies', as Murray tells us, 'four distinct varieties of Scottish glen scenery, as though here were several glens in one'. Close to the head of the Lyon River is a range of hills overlooking Rannoch Moor, with Beinn a'Chreachain (3,540 feet) the highest point. Further east Stuchd an Lochain is of interest because there is an account of an ascent in 1590 by a local chief, Mad Colin Campbell, and one of his retainers. The climb seems to have aroused some curious primitive instincts in them both for, after forcing a herd of goats over a precipice, each of them came close in turn to murdering the other by the same method. Farther down, Glen Lyon is bounded on the south by the Ben Lawers group and on the other side by the Carn Mairg range, which has several 3,000-foot peaks reminiscent of the Cairngorms.

Over towards the Tummel Valley stands the isolated quartzite cone of Schiehallion (3,547 feet), another mountain of distinctive outline prominent in the view from many a distant hill. There is very little exposed rock and it is a straightforward climb. This mountain was the scene of an elegant and important scientific experiment carried out by Maskelyne, then Astronomer Royal, in 1772. On a flat site a plumb line will hang vertically due to the attraction of the earth below; near a mountain, however, the plumb line will be deflected from the vertical by an amount proportional to the ratio between the mass of the mountain and the mass of the earth. The mass of a uniform isolated hill like Schiehallion can be easily calculated and the deflection of the plumb line in its vicinity enables the mass of the earth to be determined. Maskelyne's results were surprisingly accurate.

Through the next valley line 'by Loch Tummel and Loch Rannoch', as every schoolchild knows, runs the 'Road to the Isles'. The triangle of high country between here, Glen Garry and Loch Ericht reaches 3,306 feet at Beinn Udlamain. Above the Drumochter Pass, which carries the Perth–Inverness railway over the highest rail summit in the country, are the quaintly-named Sow of Athole and Boar of Badenoch, both around 2,500 feet.

*   *   *   *   *

The next great hill block to the east includes the high Cairngorm Mountains. It is divided into northern and southern areas by the River Dee which rises at 4,000 feet on Braeriach and flows first south, then east to the sea at Aberdeen. The majority of the mountains are of granite which was intruded through a plateau of schist, gneiss and quartzite, and many carry the characteristic tors. There are numerous fine corries and crags and these exhibit the well-known 'titanic masonry' appearance, typical of this rock elsewhere. This is the toughest walking country in Britain, presenting, in the event of bad weather, serious problems indeed in route finding and endurance. Ascents and crossings should only be attempted by the competent and well equipped. A large part of the area is a Nature Reserve and there is a National Forest Park at Glenmore.

We start with the southern group. Beside the Drumochter Pass rises the Forest of Atholl, the summit of which, Beinn Dearg, is some miles further east. To the north is Gaick Forest with extensive hydro-electric works in Glen Tromie. In 1800 an avalanche hereabouts overwhelmed a hut in which five men were sleeping; there have been other records of snow slides. The Minigaig Pass (2,750 feet), which between Blair Atholl and Kingussie is ten miles shorter than the Drumochter, is now only a drove road, though it is said that carts used to cross it at one time. The southern boundary of this area is Glen Garry, which carries the northbound road and railways towards the Drumochter Pass and Inverness. At Blair Atholl it is joined by Glen Tilt and farther on, beyond the Pass of Killiecrankie, scene of a famous battle in 1689, meets the Tummel Valley coming in from the west. South of Glen Tilt is Beinn a'Ghlo (3,671 feet), the highest point of a range of 3,000-foot peaks which stretches on north-eastwards for many miles almost to Braemar. The rocks are schist, quartzite and limestone. This is bounded on the east by the road pass from Glen Shee to Glen Clunie, the Cairnwell (2,199 feet), the highest motor road in Scotland. The famous Devil's Elbow is below the summit on the Perthshire side. The next block of hills rises around the heads of Glens Isla, Clova and Callater. Again there are numerous 3,000-foot summits, with Glas Maol (3,502 feet) the highest. Several miles to the south the detached mass of Mount Blair is believed to be the site of the battle between Agricola and the Picts in A.D. 86, the *Mons Graupius* of Tacitus.

In Balmoral Forest south of the Dee Valley rises the fine granite mass of Lochnagar—'so distinctive is its outline and so gracefully do the lower and supporting heights combine with the central mass to form a noble mountain landscape, that it is not surprising that it has become one of the most famous of Scottish hills and most popular of mountains'. The mountain gets its name from a small loch at the foot, though in early times it appeared on maps variously as Ben Chichnes or White Mounth. Byron, who spent his boyhood at Aberdeen, wrote later in life of the 'steep frowning glories of dark Lochnagar'; one of the outstanding glories is the fine display of creeping azalea which lights up acres of the summit slopes in a favourable June. In the north-east corrie is one of the most popular crags in Scotland offering a fine selection of winter and summer climbing. There is climbing too on Creag an Dubh Loch farther south.

Glen Clova is the most important of a series of valleys which run into Strathmore down the southern slopes of these hills, known as the Braes of Angus. This glen is botanically noteworthy and there is some climbing. Good tracks lead over to Glen Callater and Glen Muick; Driesh to the west is 3,105 feet. Gradually decreasing in height the hills stretch eastwards for 40 miles from Lochnagar. There is but one 3,000-foot summit, Mount Keen (3,077 feet), climbed as long ago as 1618. To the north beyond the Dee similar extensive foothills separate the highest mountains from the coastal plain. The first group of really high mountains here includes Ben Avon (3,843 feet) and Beinn a' Bhùird (3,924 feet). Ben Avon has a fine collection of summit tors with wind-eroded basins in the granite reminiscent of Dartmoor. Outstanding are the Clach Bun Rudhtair, which 'stand up like gigantic rhinoceros horns'. John Taylor, who passed this way in 1618, wrote of the mountain as—'Mount Benawne, with a furr'd mist upon his snowie head instead of a nightcap . . . the oldest man alive never saw but the snow on the top of divers of those hills, both in summer as well as in winter'. Beinn a' Bhùird was climbed by Queen Victoria and the Prince Consort in 1850. There is some rock climbing.

Adjoining to the west and higher still are the Cairngorm Mountains proper, bounded on this side by the Lairig an Laoigh, which gives a 16-mile walkers-only route from Braemar to Nethy Bridge, and on the other by Glen Feshie. There are three groups of hills. The eastern, which includes Ben Macdhui (4,296 feet), Britain's second highest mountain, and Cairn Gorm (4,084 feet), from which the whole range is named, is separated from the central group by the famous Lairig Ghru, another route for hard walkers from the Dee to the Spey. The chief summits of the central group are Braeriach (4,248 feet) and Cairn Toul (4,241 feet), while farther south is Beinn Bhrotain (3,795 feet). Between Gleann Einich and Glen Feshie the easterly group reaches 3,658 feet at Sgor Gaoith. The four 4,000-foot summits were traversed in 4 hours, 41 minutes in 1964; most of us would need rather longer than this!

Cairn Gorm, with a chairlift almost to the summit as well as a number of rope tows on the Aviemore side, is a popular ski-ing mountain. A new road up Coire Cas enables skiers to reach a height of 2,500 feet and makes the ascent in summer even easier than previously.

As long ago as 1801 the Hon. Mrs Murray found no difficulties in reaching nearly to the top on pony back; there she found the traditional hollow filled with snow never melted by rain or sun. Cairn Gorm has given its name to special quartz crystals, blue or brown in colour, which occur in veins of white quartz not only here but on other granite mountains. In MacCulloch's time these were on sale at jewellers' shops in Edinburgh, where Brazil crystal, he tells us, was passed off as local stone at 20 times its value. There is climbing in the northern corries of an t'Sneachda and an Lochain.

Ben Macdhui, variously rendered as 'hill of the black pig', 'boar-hunting ground' and 'dark hills', disputed the title of highest mountain with Ben Nevis until finally deposed by the Ordnance Survey in 1847. At one time (1819) there was a project to build a 100-foot cairn on the summit, presumably to make up what someone believed to be the difference in height, but nothing came of it. Queen Victoria climbed the mountain by pony in 1859 and, while Mr Gladstone ascended on foot in 1884, there is no record of what he said on the subject. It was in 1925 that J. N. Collie first reported in public his encounter some years previously with the spectre of Ben Macdhui—Ferlas Mor, the giant Grey Man. On his way to the summit in a mist he heard footsteps behind him in the snow, which stopped when he stopped, continued when he continued. Finally as he reached the top they began to draw nearer and nearer; 'I was seized', he said, 'with an intolerable fright and I ran my hardest down the mountainside. No power on earth will ever take me up Ben Macdhui again'. Later others, seemingly equally reliable, told of similar experiences; it is a strange affair. The more usual spectre, the Brocken, is easier to explain away. The viewer, standing with his back to the sun, sees a huge shadow of himself cast on a bank of mist. The shadow is in fact the same size as the observer but, as it is formed in depth in the mist, he associates it with ground visible at a distance and scales it accordingly. The Ben Macdhui Man with his heavy footsteps would appear to be more substantial than this.

There are several fine climbers' crags on and around the mountain, in the corries of Etchachan and Sputan Dearg, on Carn Etchachan and on the Shelter Stone Crag above Loch Avon. The last is named after a famous natural cave at its foot, typical of the shelters provided in a basic form by nature and improved to a point of habitability by man which are sometimes used nowadays by the mountaineer as bases for attacks on the crags. We find these in all parts of Britain from Sussex to Sutherland, but most plentifully here in Scotland where they are called howffs. Many of the most famous were discovered and developed during the hard times of the 1930s when young men from the industrial lowlands turned to their mountains as a relief from the monotony of a life without work. The Shelter Stone has been known for much longer, having been described as long ago as 1794 as accommodating 18 armed men. The present-day capacity is reckoned at eight to ten climbers. Off to the north-east is Bynack More, notable for carrying the highest of the local tors, the Barns of Bynack, which, rising some 400 feet below the summit, reach heights of 50 to 100 feet. The granite is weathered, into the customary rounded masses here described as 'feather beds and sofa cushions'.

To the west the Lairig Ghru, best known of the Cairngorm passes, separates the two highest mountain blocks. It links Braemar with Aviemore 27 miles away by a route consisting of 12 miles of road and 15 of hill crossing, with a summit of 2,733 feet near the Pools of Dee. This is a serious expedition in any but the best of conditions. In Glen Dee on the south side of the pass is the famous Corrour Bothy, typical of yet another class of shelter much used by mountaineers. A hut built in 1877 to house a deer watcher, it served this purpose until 1914. Subsequently abandoned, it was used in due course, unofficially, by travellers over the pass and as a base for mountaineering. The condition gradually deteriorated over the years, mainly because the internal fitments were turned into firewood. Now recently it has been repaired and restored. Similar premises, built originally in connection with deer stalking, are used today in some other parts of Scotland by walkers and climbers.

Braeriach, 'the speckled brae', and Cairn Toul, 'the hill of the barn' (or perhaps the same as Carrauntual in Ireland), in the group to the west of the Lairig Ghru are the third and fourth mountains of Britain. On the high plateau between them at over 4,000 feet the River Dee rises at the so-called Wells of Dee and plunges in a 500-foot cascade into Garbh Choire Dhaidh to the east. The rocks alongside the fall were climbed in 1810 by Dr Skene Keith and Mr Warren, one of the earliest climbing records in the country. They 'had to climb among huge rocks, varying from one to ten tuns, and to catch hold of the stones or fragments that projected, while ascending in an angle of 70 or 80 degrees'. Other climbs have been made here more recently and in Coire Bhrochain.

The east faces of Sgor Gaoith and Sgoran Dubh present a two-mile line of crags towards Glen Feshie; there is climbing. Glen Feshie, says Murray, 'bears likeness to some uninhabited valley of cis-Himalayan Tibet. The track winds through juniper groves until the glen narrows to a gorge, where the path traverses steep slopes of scree. Splintered crags rise close above, and wild screes. Landslides falling from the high ravines have swept the track and woods, tumbling great pines'.

*   *   *   *   *

The western coast of Scotland between the Great Glen and the Clyde is occupied by the mountainous county of Argyll. In the extreme south the Mull of Kintyre, hilly rather than mountainous, looks on one hand across Kilbrennan Sound to the mountains of Arran and on the other across the North Channel to the mountains of Antrim. Farther north, between here and the Crinan Canal, in the district of Knapdale, the highest point is Sliabh Gaoil (1,840 feet). The long and curving sea-loch Loch Fyne separates Knapdale from Cowal, a blunt hilly peninsula which stretches eastwards to Lochs Goil and Long. There are no 3,000-foot mountains, but many exceed 2,000 feet; around Loch Eck is part of the Argyll National Forest Park opened in 1935, the first in Britain. To the north is the district of Ardgoil lying between Hell's Glen and the River Goil on the one hand and Glens Croe and Kinglas on the other. The southerly tip between Lochs Goil and Long is known obscurely as Argyll's Bowling Green. There is nothing of the bowling green about this terrain, graphically described by one writer in 1782 as 'all possible variety of Alpine scenery with all the horror of precipice, broken craig or overhanging rock'.

Bounded on the south and west by Glens Croe, Kinglas and Fyne and stretching across the Dunbartonshire border to the shores of Loch Lomond is the Arrochar group of hills topped by Ben Ime (3,318 feet), 'butter mountain'. The outstanding hill, however, is Ben Arthur, otherwise the Cobbler (2,891 feet), the characteristic outline of which rises immediately above the head of Loch Long. It is surmounted by three rocky peaks of mica schist—'the southern a spur, the central a monolith, the northern an overhanging cliff'. The whole is said to have a fanciful resemblance to a cobbler bending over his work, but there seems to be some controversy about which item is which in the tableau. It is said that similar rocky summit tors in the Eastern Alps are often called *Schuster*, or Cobbler—the Dreischusterspitze in the Sextenthal is a notable example. Stoddart, writing in 1800, says:

> This terrific rock forms the bare summit of a huge mountain, and its nodding top so far overhangs the base as to assume the appearance of a cobbler sitting at work, from whence the country people call it—an greasaiche crom, the crooked shoemaker.

There is a great deal of climbing here and on the adjacent peaks of Beinn Narnain, Creag Tarsuinn and A'Chrois.

Though the country is substantially hilly there is no notable mountain in Argyll to the west of Loch Fyne. This area is divided by the roughly parallel Loch Awe, which stretches for 25 miles from near the sea in the south-west almost to Ben Cruachan. The boundary on the north is the line—Glen Lochy, the Pass of Brander, lower Glen Etive. The highest point here is Beinn Bhuidhe, 'the yellow mountain', a notably botanical height between Glens Fyne and Shira.

Ben Cruachan (3,689 feet) is the topmost point of an immense block of diorite mountains covering an area of 20 square miles north of the Pass of Brander. It is a mountain widely known, famous in legend and history, though the first recorded ascent, 'tedious but not difficult', was made by MacCulloch in 1811. In the fourteenth century Barbour in his 'Brus', describing a battle in the Pass of Brander, wrote — 'Crechanben . . . I trow that nocht in all Bretane ane hear hill may funding be'. Pennant (1769) looked only from below, 'it towers to a great height, its sides are shagged with wood, and its name means a great heap', while Wilkinson (1824), who with all his experience of British mountains also failed to make the ascent, was most impressed— 'for elevation, magnitude and magnificence, I do not recollect a mountain superior to Cruachan'.

To the north-east between Glens Kinglass and Strae is Beinn Eunaich (3,242 feet). These hills are mainly of granite, with gneisses and schists, but there are outcrops also of volcanic lavas, one of which on the south-east ridge of the mountain provided an early Scottish climbing problem—the Black Shoot. This was one of the earliest objectives of the members of the newly formed Scottish Mountaineering Club in the 1890s. Beyond Glen Kinglass between there and the eastern shores of Loch Etive is the Blackmount Group of granite mountains, dominated in the south by Ben Starav and Stob Coir' an Albannaich. The former, a symmetrical mountain having no less than five radiating ridges, is roamed by a legendary white hind said to bring death in her trail. The Devil, too, came this way on one occasion leaping his fire-breathing steed from here across Loch Etive to Beinn Trilleachan, where the marks of his landing are still to be seen. Here now is the district of Benderloch (Sgor na h'Ulaidh, 'the peak of the hidden treasure'), while beyond Glen Creran stretching on to Loch Linnhe is Appin where Sgurr Dearg above Ballachulish reaches 3,362 feet.

The hills of Blackmount Forest, Stob Ghabhar, Clach Leathad, and Meall a' Bhùiridh (3,626 feet) continue northwards to the Moor of Rannoch and command magnificent views across this flat, lake-strewn area of bog and moor which stretches on far into Perthshire. The huge Corrie Ba between Clach Leathad and Stob Ghabhar is the biggest in Scotland. There is snow and ice climbing hereabouts, while Meall a' Bhùiridh is an important ski-ing mountain with chairlift and ski tow.

We have now reached the very fine mountains which bound the scenic, and traditionally tragic, Glencoe. On one side are Bidean nam Bian (3,766 feet), 'the pinnacle of the hides', highest mountain in Argyll and Buachaille Etive Mor (3,345 feet), 'the shepherd of Etive', which faces out across the Moor of Rannoch. Facing these across the Glen is the long high ridge of Aonach Eagach. Both sides belong to the National Trust for Scotland, which holds a triangle with points at Kingshouse, Dalness Lodge and Clachaig. It is a deep, treeless trough, the steep side walls on either hand towering to over 3,000 feet. On a stormy day it may still appear as it did to Thomas Newte in 1791—
' . . . on each side are the most tremendous precipices I ever beheld in any part of the world. It blew a storm. Sometimes the craggy mountains were hid in black clouds, and at others, visible through the mist, which served to aggravate the gloom of this awful place, and render it truly horrible', and we are easily persuaded to agree with him that

this is indeed a fitting scene for a massacre. The rocks here, like those of North Wales and the Lake District, are volcanic lavas and provide similar conditions for summer rock climbing. This, taken in conjunction with the wide range of winter mountaineering also available, makes Glencoe (only two hours incidentally from Glasgow) one of Scotland's leading climbing centres.

Bidean nam Bian is in fact a mountain range with 12 miles of high ridges and nine summits. Three of them, Beinn Fhada, Gearr Aonach and Aonach Dubh, forming the south wall of Glencoe, are called the Three Sisters. High up in the face of Aonach Dubh is Ossian's Cave, a tall black slit resembling a large keyhole. It was first reached by a local shepherd in 1868 up a steep climb of rock and vegetation known as Ossian's Ladder. Actually there is little of a cave about the place, which is only a few feet deep with the floor at an angle of 45 degrees, damp and depressing. Buachaille Etive Mor is a steep cone of black rock rising in the acute angle between Glencoe and Glen Etive. In the early morning the level rays of the sun shining across the flat expanse of the Moor of Rannoch light up the rocks or the snows of the eastern face often with startling effects. The Moor has an area of between 50 and 60 square miles in the triangle Loch Tulla, Kingshouse Inn and Loch Rannoch. The highest point is 1,795 feet, the lowest 540 feet, but it is remarkably flat; one can walk it is said, in a straight line for ten miles between the 950- and 1,000-foot contours. There are mountains all around, Blackmount and Buachaille Etive on one side, Beinn Achaladair, Ben a' Chreachain and the hills of north-west Perthshire on the second and the Black Corries on the third. The road from Bridge of Orchy to Glencoe skirts the south-western edge, but the West Highland Railway, protected by avalanche sheds, strikes straight across. There are small remnants here of the Great Wood of Caledon which formerly covered large areas of Scotland—the Black Wood near Loch Rannoch, another wood on the south side of Loch Tulla and Crannog Wood near the railway. It is Scotland's biggest and most colourful moor, far removed from Lettice's view (1792)—'an immense vacuity, with nothing in it to contemplate, unless number-less misshapen blocks of stone rising hideously above the surface of the earth'.

*   *   *   *   *

183

The long straight trough of the Great Glen, a major geological fault line which demarcates this area on the north, is occupied for most of its length by Lochs Linnhe, Lochy and Ness, the last 750 feet deep and complete with famous monster. At the western end Fort William lies at the head of the sea-loch Linnhe where it swings round through more than a right angle into Loch Eil, and four miles east-south-east is Ben Nevis, the highest point in these islands. The summit is 4,406 feet above sea level, and, as has been said, less than 1,000 feet below the permanent snow-line for this latitude under present climatic conditions. We are thus not very far from having small glaciers on some of our northern mountains. Certainly some banks of snow in north-facing gullies only disappear in exceptional years; indeed in the last century, when conditions were somewhat colder than now, some of these beds were believed to be permanent. It is interesting, too, to note that only a few thousand years ago much of this mountain area was ice covered.

Ben Nevis takes the form, very familiar in Britain, of a half plum pudding, the convex slopes running down into Glen Nevis on the west and south, the steep face into the Allt a' Mhuilinn to the north-east. The ascent from Glen Nevis is straightforward by a track built originally to serve the Summit Observatory. The north ridge is prolonged by the adjacent summit of Carn Dearg (3,961 feet) which contributes substantially to the vast scale of the north-easterly precipice. This is by far the most impressive crag face in Britain, about two miles long and in places almost 2,000 feet high and offering summer and winter climbing of every type and standard. On the far side of the Allt a' Mhuilinn is Carn Mor Dearg (4,012 feet) and beyond this the summits of the Aonachs, where the Beag (4,060 feet) is higher than the Mor (3,999 feet); presumably it is greater bulk which determines the name. Glen Nevis bounds all these various hills on their southern sides; it is a remarkable valley, 'in parts', says W. H. Murray, 'Himalayan in character and one of the scenic wonders of Scotland'. Beyond are the bold and rocky hills of the Mamore Forest (Binnein Mor, 3,700 feet). Between the Aonachs and Loch Trieg are the Grey Corries—two groups of hills each with a peak called Stob Coire Easain. The easterly one at 3,658 feet is the highest of its group, but the westerly group culminates in Stob Choire Claurigh (3,858 feet).

A number of derivations have been suggested for the name 'Nevis', all of them entertaining and imaginative. From a word meaning 'venom' we get the interesting possibility of 'the wild, fierce, horrid, venomous ben' or, maybe, it is Beinn Neanh-bhathain, 'the sky-touching mountain', or from 'nimh uisg', 'biting cold water'. The authorities cannot seem to agree.

Fort William received its name in 1690 and soon became firmly established on maps, yet the Ben, on its very doorstep, remained unrecognized for almost another century. Finally in Faden's Atlas (1778) it appears faintly disguised as 'Ben Nevish'. Dorett (1782) wrote 'Ben Nevist' and Campbell (1790), proudly, 'Ben Nivis the Highest Mtn. in Britain'. Others of Scotland's mountains had figured from time to time on earlier maps, for example Tacitus wrote of *Mons Graupius* from which the word Grampian was probably derived, but usually there was little stability of site or spelling and mistakes were seldom corrected. This is of course in no way surprising in such wild and remote country, where a mountain might easily have different names on its various sides.

Even before it appeared on the maps the mountain was known to be one of the highest in the land and for this reason was sometimes climbed. In the 1720s one such attempt was made on 'this mountain in Lochaber of three quarters of a mile of perpendicular height' by fellow officers of that subordinate of General Wade, the letter-writing Captain Burt:

> This wild expedition in ascending round and round the hills, in finding accessible places, in helping one another up the rocks, in disappointments, and their returning to the foot of the mountain, took them up a whole summer day, from five o'clock in the morning.

Had they been caught in the mist, he adds, 'there would have been no means left for them to find their way down, and they must have perished with cold, wet, and hunger'.

Thomas Pennant, the travelling Welsh squire, who came this way in the 1760s, was saddened to learn that his own Snowdon 'once esteemed the highest hill in the island must now yield the palm to a Caledonian mountain'. As elsewhere, this was the period when attitudes were changing rapidly. In the middle of the century one of Cumberland's soldiers, encamped locally, tells of the 'hypochondriacal melancholy' induced by the surrounding mountains, yet 50 years later Cririe's view was quite different: 'The traveller who can behold them and not feel a sense of the greatness and majesty of the Almighty impressed on his heart, must be strangely devoid of taste and sentiment.'

Thomas Wilkinson, always attracted by the mountains in his path, visited Fort William in 1797. Unable to find a guide in the town he tackled the mountain solo; unfortunately his narrative does not make it clear whether he reached the top, though he certainly seems to have looked down the great northern precipices:

> The north side of the mountain may be said to be hung with terror. Perpendicular and projecting rocks, gulphy glens and awful precipices, gloomy and tremendous caverns, the vast repositories of snow from age to age; these, with blue mists gauzing the grey rocks of the mountain, and terrible cataracts thundering from Ben Nevis, made altogether a scene sublimely dreadful.

The sovereignty of Scotland's mountains, in dispute for many a year between Ben Nevis and Ben Macdhui, was finally accorded to the former by the Ordnance Survey in 1847. The following year came the first of the mountaineers, Professor Forbes, who cut the first step in Scottish snow during a three-day circuit of the mountain.

During the 1880s the summit of Ben Nevis became the site of an important meteorological experiment. The pioneer was Clement Wragge who in the summers of 1881 and 1882 climbed the mountain almost daily, a round trip of 14 miles, and made observations in a stone hut on the summit. This was replaced by an Observatory 13 feet square opened in October, 1883, to which was added the following year a further room and a tower. Later another building was erected some 50 yards away to provide refreshments and sleeping accommodation for travellers. Observations were made here continuously until lack of funds forced a shut-down in 1904. The ruins of the buildings remain. It was a tough life for the observers; as Professor Manley has said: ' . . . the impression gained by anyone who has to sojourn for one purpose or another on our high summits is likely to be one of pitiless and nearly incessant raw cold wind and a great deal of low cloud, with abundant rime deposit throughout the winter.' These rime deposits sometimes reached lengths of five feet, they found; there was snow cover for 215 days in the year; snow or sleet fell on 169 days with a total annual rainfall of 157 inches; the sun shone for a mere 750 hours in the year and the average temperature in the warmest month only reached 41° F. These inhabited buildings provided excellent shelter for travellers and many more were thereby encouraged to tackle the ascent. Mountaineers coming up the north face were welcomed with hot drinks, though a party was once told—'Had you come here on the Lord's Day you would not have gained admittance'.

The summit was reached during the Observatory period by a motor-cyclist and later, in 1911, by car. The venturesome motorist, aided by a gang of workmen, proceeded over bogs from Inverlochy to Half Way House and thence by bridle path. He did not, we are told, 'confine himself to the track and in parts drove his car over the thickly strewn porphyry stones'. Higher up there was trouble with the snow and 'dashes had to be made over bare patches composed entirely of rough boulders' before the top was reached. The bridle path was an encouragement to record making. In 1895 William Swann covered the summit and back from Fort William in 2 hours 41 minutes. After several more solo attempts a race was organized in 1899 under A.A.A. Rules. Between 1903 and 1937 there was no contest but since then it has become an almost annual event. In 1954 Brian Kearney recorded 1 hour 49 minutes, while for the ladies Kathleen Connochie did 3 hours 2 minutes in 1955.

*   *   *   *   *

Between the Great Glen to the north and the line Glen Spean–Strathspey is a wide area of schistose mountains stretching up to Inverness and beyond. In Glen Roy above Roy Bridge are the famous 'Parallel Roads', a series of shelves round the hillsides marking successive positions of the shores of an ancient lake, held back by an ice barrier. There are three distinct shelves at 855, 1,067 and 1,148 feet. Among a group of rounded hills above Loch Laggan is Creag Meaghaidh (3,700 feet). There are several steep-sided corries; Coire Ardair in particular has provided winter climbing of a high standard as well as 'unorthodox rock and vegetable work' in the summer. This is the sort of place which prompted a well-known climber to assert: 'Any fool can climb good rock, but it takes craft and cunning to get up vegetatious schist or granite'. Farther north-east are the extensive Monadhliath, 'grey moors', separated from Creag Meaghaidh by the famous Pass of Corrieyairack (2,543 feet). General Wade built a road through here in 1731 but it was already an important communication link between the Great Glen and the south and had been used by Montrose and his troops nearly a century before. Henry Skrine, who crossed in a carriage in 1793, wrote afterwards: ' . . . inexpressibly arduous road . . . elevated to a height truly terrific — springing sometimes from point to point over alpine bridges and at other times pursuing narrow ridges of rock frightfully impending over tremendous precipices'. Unfortunately it is not that exciting, the hills are featureless, though the summit view helps to compensate. The road is completely neglected nowadays.

Farther south between Loch Trieg, Loch Laggan and Loch Ericht are the Corrour and Ben Alder Forests, another 'region of outstanding beauty'. Ben Alder (3,757 feet) is of schist capped with granite and among several other 3,000-foot mountains are Beinn Eibhinn, 'the beautiful mountain', and Geal Charn, an extensive plateau having on its eastern edge a peak, Sgor Iutharn, said to look from some points of view even sharper than the Matterhorn. The pass between Geal Charn and Ben Alder, the Bealach Dubh, marks the line of a notable long-distance walk—the ascent of all Scotland's 4,000-foot summits in one expedition. These peaks, which are divided between the Ben Nevis group and the Cairngorms some 55 miles apart, were first traversed in the 1920s with the help of a car. It was not until 1954 that the whole expedition was done on foot by Frank Williamson, who took 50 hours from Fort William to Glenmore Lodge. The walking route between the areas runs from Glen Nevis past the head of Loch Treig, beside Loch Ossian, up the long valley of Uisge Labhair, over the Bealach Dubh and down by Loch Pattack to Loch Ericht, then by road to Dalwhinnie and on into Cairngorm country.

27 *Slioch from Loch Mare*

TEN

Scottish Highlands
and Islands

The district called the Western Highlands, which lies between the Great Glen, the Dingwall to Kyle of Lochalsh railway and the western seaboard, is divided by a series of valleys which run substantially from east to west. The major part of it is Inverness-shire, the remainder Ross and Cromarty. Six of Murray's 'regions of outstanding beauty' are included—three of them the contiguous areas of Knoydart, Glenelg and Kintail along the coast opposite Skye, Moidart farther south and the inland valleys of Loch Arkaig and Glen Affric. The rock types are varied and the geology complex; there is little rock climbing but mile upon mile of rounded mountainsides, blotted here and there by hydro-electric activities.

Bonnie Prince Charlie hid in this part of the Highlands for some half of the five months which elapsed between Culloden and his final escape to France. In the battle, fought on 16 April, 1746, the issue was settled within half an hour; the Pretender fled westwards and on 26 April sailed from Loch nan Uamh in Morar. After sundry adventures in the Outer Isles and in Skye he landed on the mainland once again on 5 July. Thenceforward, until he finally made his getaway from Loch nan Uamh on 19 September, he spent his time wandering and hiding among the peaks and glens looking and waiting for a means of escape to be revealed. With various companions he slept out in caves and in the open, was mercilessly hunted over hillsides and passes, yet surprisingly was never betrayed.

South of the Mallaig railway in a huge peninsula facing the Isle of Mull are the districts of Morven, Ardnamurchan, Moidart, Sunart and Ardgour. Morven in the south-west corner is separated from the

28 *Beinn Dearg and Strath na*
Sheallag, Ross-shire

rest by Loch Sunart and Glen Tarbert, above which is Creach Bheinn, its highest point. To the north Ardnamurchan is the most westerly point of the mainland of Great Britain, projecting, surprisingly, 20 miles west of Land's End. The hills make up for their lack of height by extreme ruggedness. This is the site of a once great volcano and abounds in igneous rocks. Beinn na Seilg is of gabbro like the rocks of Skye; Ben Hiant, the highest point, is diorite. Sunart and Ardgour form a diamond-shaped wedge of country between Lochs Sheil and Linnhe. A series of peaks, exhibiting Gaelic at its most tongue-twisting in Sgor Craobh a'Chaoruinn, Meall an Doire Shleaghaich, etc., culminates in Sgurr Dhomhnuill (2,915 feet). Garbh Bheinn, a craggy quartzite mountain north of Glen Tarbert, is very shapely and offers some fine rock climbing. Farther west Ben Resipol rises in comparative isolation between Lochs Sheil and Sunart. At the head of Loch Sheil is Glenfinnan where Bonnie Prince Charlie first raised his standard at the beginning of the '45 rising. Between here and the sea is Moidart, mountainous in the north, with Rois-bheinn (2,876 feet) the highest point and a Beinn Odhar Bheag 42 feet higher than Beinn Odhar Mhor nearby.

Between Loch Eil and Loch Arkaig is Locheil Forest (Gulvain, 3,224 feet). The mountains near the Great Glen are rounded and dull but the Streaps above Glenfinnan are steep and fine. The line of hills continues by Sgurr Thuilm and Sgurr nan Coireachan into Morar. Here the mountains are lesser but the views open up along the coast and across to the islands. This district is divided into two by the long narrow Loch Morar, which reaches the extraordinary depth of 1,080 feet, and is bounded in the north by the beautiful sea-loch Nevis. This is the gateway to the exceedingly wild and rugged district of Knoydart, 'the Rough Bounds of Knoydart', which stretches from here to Loch Hourn. The remote schistose peak of Ladhar Bheinn (3,343 feet) is the highest hereabouts. The eastward valley line from the head of Loch Hourn runs by Loch Quoich and Glen Garry back to the Great Glen, enclosing another huge hill mass between here and the line Loch Nevis–Loch Arkaig. This is topped by the striking Sgurr na Ciche (3,410 feet) near the head of Loch Nevis.

The mountain area immediately to the north is bounded in turn by the valley line, Glen Shiel–Glen Cluanie–Glen Moriston. A

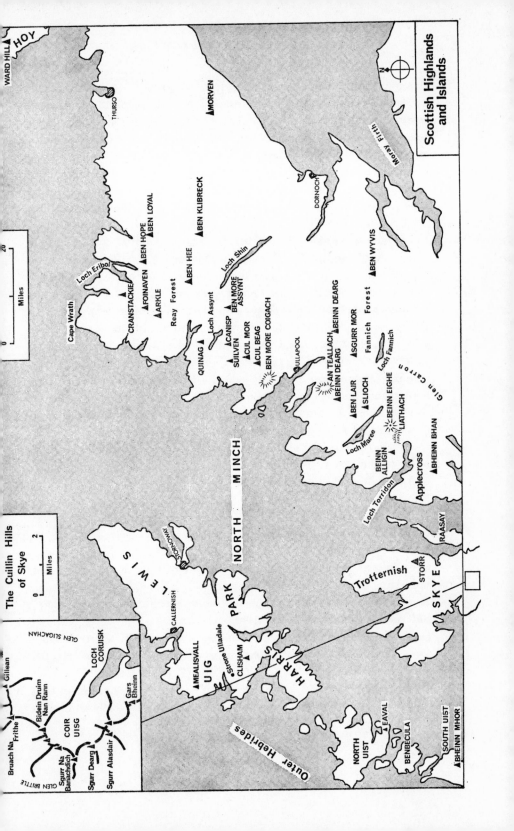

Scottish Highlands and Islands

HOY
▲WARD HILL

THURSO

▲MORVEN

Cape Wrath
Loch Eribol
CRANSTACKIE▲
▲FOINAVEN ▲BEN HOPE
▲ARKLE ▲BEN LOYAL
Reay Forest
▲BEN HEE
▲BEN KLIBRECK

DORNOCH

Moray Firth

QUINAG▲
Loch Assynt
Loch Shin
BEN MORE
ASSYNT
▲CANISP
SUILVEN▲
▲CUL MOR
▲CUL BEAG
▲BEN MORE COIGACH

ULLAPOOL

Loch Maree
AN TEALLACH▲
BEINN DEARG▲
BEINN DEARG▲
▲SGURR MOR
Fannich Forest
Loch Fannich
▲BEN WYVIS

▲BEN LAIR
▲SLIOCH
BEINN EIGHE▲
LIATHACH▲
Glen Carron

BEINN BHAN▲
BEINN
ALLIGIN
Applecross
Loch Torridon

RAASAY

Trotternish
STORR▲
SKYE

NORTH MINCH

STORNOWAY
LEWIS
PARK
UIG
●Stone Ulladale
CALLERNISH
CLISHAM
▲MEALISVALL
HARRIS

Outer Hebrides

NORTH UIST
BENBECULA
EAVAL▲
SOUTH UIST
▲BHEINN MHOR

Miles
0   20

The Cuillin Hills of Skye

Miles
0   2

GLEN SLIGACHAN
LOCH CORUISK
Gars Bheinn▲

Bruach Na
Frithe▲
Gillean▲
Bidein Druim
Nan Rann▲
Sgurr Na
Banachdich▲
COIR
UISG
Sgurr Dearg▲
Sgurr Alasdair▲
GLEN BRITTLE

notable feature here is the seven-mile ridge of Aonach air Chrith (3,342 feet); there are several more 3,000-foot summits southwards towards Loch Quoich, while in the west the shapely Saddle (3,317 feet) (why an English name?) is a fine mountain indeed. 'Its summit ridges', says Murray, 'dwindle to knife edges and burst in pinnacles, its corries show ice worn rock, its flanks are precipitous; the summit is a thin ridge slung between two peaks'. Further on Ben Sgriol has a fine view over the straits to Skye and into Loch Hourn down a drop of 3,200 feet in a mile.

Facing the Saddle across Glen Shiel is a six-mile chain of peaks, 'the Five Sisters of Kintail' (Sgurr Fhuaran, 3,505 feet), and to the east of this between Glen Affric and Glen Cluanie is a vast area of mountains, smooth, rounded and rockless with several 3,000-foot summits topped by A'Chràlaig (3,673 feet). The next peak to the east is Sgurr nan Conbhairean, near the summit of which Bonnie Prince Charlie spent a July night 'wet to the skin and devoured by midges'. A few miles away in Coire Mheadhoin below Tigh Mor na Seilge, 'the big house of the hunting', he hid for more than a week in a large natural cave among a pile of boulders. His trials and struggles belong to sterner times; he can only have loathed mountains, good as they were as hiding places. Caves of this type still serve, however, as shelters for mountain travellers of a later age. The high ground continues for many miles to the east right up to Loch Ness.

At the head of Glen Affric is the ridge of Beinn Fhada (3,383 feet), 'the long mountain', often called Ben Attow. It is a seven-mile ridge with four miles above 2,750 feet. A stream on its north side flows into Glen Elchaig over the Falls of Glomach, which at 350 feet are the highest in Scotland. North of Glen Affric are the highest mountains in the Western Highlands, the twin summits of Carn Eige (3,877 feet) and Mam Sodhail (3,862 feet), separated by a half-mile length of ridge. These in common with many of the mountains hereabouts are smooth and rounded schistose formations with little in the way of exposed rock. The summits are remote but the ascents are easy. Facing them across Glen Cannich rises Sgurr na Lapaich (3,773 feet) the summit of a long range dividing Glen Cannich from Glen Strathfarrar. An Riabhachan, close by, is the highest mountain in Ross-shire. Because of their isolated positions commanding views from the Outer Hebrides to the

Cairngorms and from Sutherland to Perthshire, Mam Sodhail and Sgurr na Lapaich were important stations in the Ordnance Survey triangulation of Britain in the 1840s. Large cairns recall these map-making activities. The charm of this district resided at one time in the great glens of Strathfarrar, Cannich and Affric, once among the most beautiful in Scotland. The mountains are a background to the scenery of the valleys, which have of late years suffered much disfigurement from hydro-electric and forestry activities.

Beyond Glen Strathfarrar are the most northerly ranges of the Western Highlands in the Forests of Monar, Strathconon and Glen Carron. There are two groups of hills, the eastern topped by Sgurr a Choire Ghlais, the western by Sgurr a'Chaorachain—smooth, featureless with very little exposed rock and, of course, very remote. The hills of Glen Carron Forest look down on Glen Carron and the Dingwall–Kyle railway and across to the Northern Highlands beyond.

*   *   *   *   *

The Northern Highlands, in the counties of Caithness, Sutherland and Ross and Cromarty, are bounded on the south by the valleys of Glen Carron, Strath Bran and Strath Conon. Over most of the area the mountains are divided by a series of valleys running from south-east to north-west, except in the far north where the rivers flow towards the north coast. Before describing in detail the complex tangle of mountains with which the district is almost entirely covered, we take a look first at the predominating rock types.

In the extreme west the hills rest on a platform of gneiss, an ancient rock which mostly forms rough, lake-strewn (and midge-infested) moors, yet sometimes reaches to summits notably at Ben More Assynt, Letterewe Forest and A'Mhaighdean. Above this bed of gneiss rise the magnificent Torridon Sandstone mountains, characteristic of this part of the Highlands, which stretch from Bheinn Bhàn in Applecross to Quinag above Kylesku. The rock is purple in colour and hori-zontally bedded forming steep wall-like crags often many miles long with rounded buttresses and pinnacled ridges above. Some of the Torridonian peaks have a capping of whitish quartzite, which has helped to preserve the sandstone from denudation. The striking change of form and colour between these two rock types can occasionally be seen dividing a huge crag, notably on the 1,300-foot face of Beinn Eighe above Coire Mhic Fhearchair. Farther north in Reay Forest the quartzite makes whole mountains. Close to Inchnadamph and again at Durness there are narrow bands of limestone with characteristic vegetation and a few minor caves. East of a line from Achnashellach in Glen Carron to Loch Eriboll in the far north is a great area of, so-called, Moine rocks, mostly schists and gneisses. These form the highest mountains hereabouts, but they are not so interesting to look upon or to climb as those farther west. In the east there is Old Red Sandstone above the schists and in Caithness this forms the peak of Morven as well as some high sea-cliffs.

Lying between the sea-lochs of Kishorn and Torridon in the extreme south-west of the Northern Highlands area is the peninsula of Applecross, looking over the sea to Skye. This is one of Murray's 'regions of outstanding beauty'; in fact five of these regions extend one after the other for 40 miles north-eastwards from here to Dundonnell. The highest point in Applecross is Bheinn Bhàn (2,936 feet); nearby is one of the highest motor roads in Scotland, from Kishorn to Applecross, which reaches 2,054 feet at Bealach na Bà. The mountains are Torridonian and take the form of a flat plateau sloping gently to the west, but having a 1,200-foot face of purple sandstone to the east. There are four big corries—one of them, Coire na Poite, flanked with rock spurs which terminate, as the guidebook tells us, in 'huge round masses of rock, known as A'Chioch and A'Poite, whose perpendicular sides and horizontal lines of stratification, like courses of Cyclopean masonry, suggest the idea of Titanic castles, habitations for the giants . . . '. Rock climbing has been done here, some of reasonably high standard.

Torridonian Sandstone is very different from the volcanic rocks on which most British climbs are made. The vertical lines of weakness which predominate on the latter provide the climber with his routes—natural ways up the crag demarcated by more difficult rocks on either side which leave little possibility for diversion. This Highland sandstone, however, is sedimentary; horizontal lines of weakness are plentiful and vertical lines few, so that the crag often appears like a series of outcrops one above the other and the climber can vary his point of attack for each of them. Thus his final line is often a zigzag.

It is unlikely therefore that a network of routes will ever be made on these crags comparable with those on other rock types; they are safeguarded, too, by difficulties of access in this somewhat remote terrain.

East of Loch Damh and between Glens Carron and Torridon are the Ben Damh and Coulin Forests; among about a dozen mountains of Torridonian Sandstone, some capped with quartzite, Sgorr Ruadh is the highest. This area is bounded on the north by Glen Torridon, of which Murray has said: 'the glen, its loch and the mountains to either side exhibit more of mountain beauty than any other district of Scotland, including Skye'. Perhaps the finest of the surrounding mountains is the grand five-mile ridge of Liathach, extremely steep not only on this side but on the north also. This is a mountain range with six summits over 3,000 feet, Torridonian Sandstone again with quartzite caps. Spidean a'Choire Leith (3,456 feet), 'peak of the grey corrie', is the highest. There is rock climbing here, while in winter due to the steepness of the slopes even the easiest route to the summit may present considerable difficulties.

As we move westwards the next mountain is Beinn Alligin, which has similar steep crags and a magnificent summit view extending along the western seaboard from Ardnamurchan to Cape Wrath. This is the western end of a range of hills which runs parallel to the ridge of Liathach, through Beinn Dearg to Beinn Eighe (3,309 feet) above Kinlochewe. Between here and Loch Maree are the wilds of Shieldaig and Flowerdale Forests. Beinn Eighe again is a mountain range with seven 3,000-foot peaks of which Ruadh Stac Mor is the highest. The eastern summits are predominantly quartzite but on those to the west and the north the quartzite caps massive bastions of Torridonian Sandstone. The great crags in Coire Mhic Fhearchair, to which we have already referred, form one of the finest precipices in Scotland; some climbs have been made but, as it takes a long walk to reach them, many prospects remain.

Loch Maree, stretching 12 miles north-westwards from Kinlochewe to a point only two miles short of the sea, is perhaps the finest inland lake in the country. The mountains on the north shore are mostly of gneiss and these we will discuss later. The line of the sandstone continues with the Slioch (3,217 feet) above the head of the lake, where the Torridonian rests on a bed of gneiss, Mullach Coire Mhic Fhearchair (3,326 feet), where sandstone, gneiss and quartzite are mixed in a complex fashion, and on to another Beinn Dearg, this one rising above Strath na Sheallag. Beyond the strath is the third great range of Torridonian peaks—An Teallach—with more than a dozen 3,000-foot points on a two-mile ridge. The highest, Bidean a'Ghlas Thuill (3,483 feet), 'the sharp pointed peak of the grey hollow', rises at the head of a spur separating the huge cliffy corries of a 'Ghlas Thuill and Toll an Lochain. Pennant, when passing this way, was specially impressed:

> To the west is a view where the awful, or rather the horrible, predominates—a chain of rocky mountains with sides dark, deep and precipitous; with summits broken, sharp, and serrated, and springing into all terrific forms; with snowy glaciers lodged in the deep shaded apertures. . . .

A few years later MacCulloch climbed An Teallach during his Tour.

Along the west coast of Ross and Sutherland between Ullapool and Kylesku are a series of mountains of remarkable shape, pyramids and cocked-hat ridges of Torridonian Sandstone resting on a platform of gneiss, and looking, MacCulloch tells us, 'as if they had been shaken down at random out of a pepper pot'. Stac Polly (2,009 feet) has a long summit ridge of sandstone pinnacles with steep scree slopes on either hand, resembling, as Professor Heddle once said, 'a porcupine in a state of extreme irascibility'. A traverse of this mountain is an interesting and photogenic rock climb. Six miles north-east Suilven (2,399 feet) is similarly constructed—a triple peaked ridge, one and a half miles long, presenting a conical outline at one end and a steeply domed effect at the other. Again a traverse makes a fine expedition but the difficulty is concentrated in the ascent of the face of Caisteal Liath at the western end. These are outstanding, yet there are several others worthy of mention—Cul Mor (2,786 feet), twin cones capped with quartzite, Cul Beag (2,523 feet), Ben More Coigach (2,438 feet) and Quinag (2,653 feet); the last two are both miniature mountain ranges. MacCulloch climbed Cul Beag, while a sailor in his party reached the top of Suilven, but Professor Ramsay's ascent of the face of Caisteal Liath in 1895, 'a perfect Matterhorn', was treated locally, as he tells us, with 'consternation, incredulity, delight and a mixed state of indignation and enthusiasm'. Stac Polly and Suilven are included in one of Murray's 'regions of outstanding beauty'.

This is the end of the sandstone and we now turn back to look at the mountains in Letterewe and Fisherfield Forests, which lie between Loch Maree and Strath na Sheallag. These give some of the best of the local rock climbing for the rock is sound and gives routes comparable with those on volcanic crags. Ben Lair (2,817 feet) throws down on its north-east side above Gleann Tùlacha a two-and-a-half-mile face of hornblende-schist, on which, as late as 1951, no climbs had yet been recorded. Suddenly it was extensively explored by several independent parties with results extremely puzzling to guidebook writers:

> Although the Glasgow pioneers have identified their Molar, Angel and Wisdom Buttresses with the Peak, Overhang and Cigar Buttresses of the subsequent party, and several routes on the first of these are obviously distinct, there may be much overlap in the routes on the other buttresses owing to the brevity of the descriptions and complexity of rock formation.

A year or two later great gneiss crags on Beinn a'Chàisgein Mor and Sgurr na Laocainn above Fionn Loch were opened up, so that altogether this is perhaps the finest rock climbing area in the Northern Highlands. For the mountain traveller Murray describes this as a 'mountainous maze, in appearance rather than in fact, not paralleled elsewhere in its savage complexity'. The highest of these hills of gneiss is A'Mhaighdean (3,100 feet), 'the maiden', which lies three and a half miles north of Slioch. Much farther north above Inchnadamph the gneiss reaches its maximum elevation at Ben More Assynt (3,273 feet), the highest mountain in Sutherland.

The main schistose hills begin at Fionn Bheinn (3,060 feet) immediately north of Achnasheen. This looks down on to Loch Fannich, beyond which rise the high hills of Fannich Forest—a nine-mile ridge reaching 3,637 feet at Sgurr Mor, the highest point in the Northern Highlands. This is a fine group for walking but there is little rock exposed. Many miles farther east Ben Wyvis (3,429 feet), 'the awesome mountain', rises in isolation close to Beauly Firth. It is a tableland three miles by six, with several summits exceeding 3,000 feet, and commands an extensive view though with a dull foreground. North of the Garve to Ullapool road is a large and somewhat featureless hill group which culminates in yet another Beinn Dearg (3,547 feet).

Sgurr nan Gillean, Skye

From here almost trackless hill country stretches eastwards and south-eastwards for many miles almost to the North Sea Coast. The feature-less schist hills continue northwards, lower now, though Beinn Leoid, between Lochs Glencoul and Merkland, is 2,597 feet.

Beyond the line Loch Shin to Loch Laxford Ben Klibreck (3,154 feet) and Ben Hee are schistose, but farther north-west are the quartzite mountains of Reay Forest—Arkle and Foinaven (2,980 feet), a range with fine peaks, which extends northwards between Strath Dionard and Loch Eriboll to Cranstackie and Beinn Spionnaidh. To the east the schist reaches 3,040 feet at Ben Hope, the farthest north of the Munros, while Ben Laoghal (Ben Loyal) nearby is an isolated granite laccolite. Both these derive stature from their isolated positions. Lesser mountains and moorlands stretch on into Caithness, wild, remote and little visited, while in many places this northern coastline falls away in stupendous sea-cliffs.

*   *   *   *   *

We now leave the mainland and turn to the numerous islands which are scattered the length of Scotland's western and northern seaboards.

The Island of Arran, 20 miles by 9 miles, which dominates the Clyde Estuary has been described 'as a geological epitome of the World' because of the large numbers of rock formations found there within a limited space. The highland line passes across the Island separating rocks and plants typical of the Highlands in the north from sandstone and volcanic rocks similar to those of southern Scotland in the south. The highest mountains, north of this line, are of granite and comprise three ridge systems radiating north, south-east and south-west from Cir Mhor (2,618 feet), 'the great comb'. Between the first two is Glen Sannox, between the second and the third Glen Rosa and com-pleting the circle Glen Iorsa. The highest point, Goatfell (2,866 feet), actually derived from Gaoth Bhein, 'hill of the wind', on the south-east ridge is believed to have been climbed by one Lugless Willie Lithgow as long ago as 1628. He describes the Island as:

> . . . sur-clouded with Goatfieldhill which with wide eyes overlooked the western continent, and the northern country of Ireland; bringing also into sight in a clear summer's day, the Isle of Man and the higher coast of Cumberland. A larger prospect no mountain in the world can show, pointing out three Kingdoms at one sight . . .

During the early part of the nineteenth century most travellers found the climb a terrifying experience; this, for example, is the Rev. T. Grierson:

The upper part of the mountain, as well as those adjoining, consists of naked rocks, huge masses of granite, piled up in the most grotesque and fantastic forms by nature's mighty architect. In some instances there is an appearance of regularity, Cyclopean walls, like mason work upon a gigantic scale. In other parts the most frightful chasms appear, into which the eye cannot penetrate without a thrill of horror, while around you are seen serrated ridges, like huge devouring fangs.

On the ridge running north is the second highest mountain— Caisteal Abhail (2,817 feet), 'the stronghold of the ptarmigan', often known as the 'Castles' because of the great rock tors on the summit, while on the third ridge Beinn Tarsuinn, 'the transverse mountain', reaches 2,706 feet. It adds to the confusion when we learn that there are four other mountains on the Island bearing this name. The walking is straightforward and the crags easily avoidable. The traverse of the A'Chir ridge between Cir Mhor and Beinn Tarsuinn, however, presents some tricky problems; in far-off 1892 during the earliest climbing exploration a piton was used in one place here. The actual summit of Ceum na Caillich, 'the Witches Step', is also difficult of access. The crags themselves are of the typical granite formation that we have seen elsewhere, variously described as 'wool packs', 'boiler plates' or 'Cyclopean walls'. Of the climbing, H. MacRobert has written:

Clasping gigantic holds with outstretched arms, squirming round and over impossible corners, shuffling up great slabs set on edge, here defying gravitation with legs jammed securely, there spreadeagled helplessly, every square inch of cuticle and Harris tweed plastered to the gritty slab—truly, the rock enthusiast among these grey peaks gets his full meed of exercise.

Farther west another granite group reaches 2,368 feet at Beinn Bharrain, while south of the line the highest hill is A'Chruach (1,679 feet). Of the other Clyde islands only the steep cone of Ailsa Craig (1,114 feet) reaches any considerable height. It is of volcanic origin and is surrounded by steep basalt sea-cliffs.

*   *   *   *   *

The Inner Hebrides stretch from the Oa of Islay to the Quirang of Skye. Islay has a lowland character though the eastern quartzite hills reach 1,609 feet at Beinn Bheigeir. Beyond the Straits of Jura the island of Jura is, by contrast, Highland with large areas of barren moorland. The famous Paps of Jura (Beinn an Oir, 2,571 feet, 'hill of gold') were climbed by MacCulloch in the early nineteenth century. These also are quartzite with long slopes of whitish scree. Between Jura and Scarba is the Gulf of Corryvreckan, where a formidable whirlpool, the 'Scottish Maelstrom', is often formed in suitable conditions of wind and tide. Scarba is a moorland dome rising to 1,470 feet.

The large island of Mull, lying off the coast of Morven and Ardnamurchan, is well wooded and full of bird-life. Ben More (3,169 feet), basalt capped with granite, is the only Munro in the islands outside Skye, MacCulloch climbed this in a hailstorm and his whisky, diluted with hail, suddenly became a mass of ice. This perhaps is why he described Mull as a 'detestable island, trackless and repulsive, rude without beauty, stormy, rainy, and dreary, a heap of rude mountains . . . an entire mass of trap rocks'. There are many more hills of over 2,000 feet in all sorts of rock types. South-eastern Mull in particular shows great variety; this area is all that remains of a volcano once 15,000 feet high. The island has 250 miles of coastline, considerably indented, and there are many fine sea-cliffs. Off the south-western corner is the holy island of Iona, where St Columba lived in the sixth century. He came from Ireland and this is commemorated in the name of a hill near the landing place—Càrn Cùll Ri Eirinn, 'the Cairn with its back to Ireland'. The rock is gneiss and reaches 332 feet at Dùn I. There are sea-cliffs and a traverse like that on Sark.

Eigg, seven miles west of Arisaig Point, is topped by the strange shape of the Scuir of Eigg (1,289 feet). End on, this appears as a steep rock tower, but it is actually the end of a long steep-sided ridge. The summit carries signs of ancient fortifications. Five miles north-west, Rum is a platform of Torridonian Sandstone 500 to 1,000 feet high. On this, in the south-east corner of the island, rests a mountain range of gabbro, quartz-felsite and granite, called, as in Skye, the Cuillin and having, also like Skye, a peak called Sgurr nan Gillean. The highest point is Askival (2,659 feet); many of the hills have similar distinctive names of Norse origin. The traverse of the ridges, first recorded by

Munro of the 'Munros' in 1891, though a fine expedition, is straight-forward and not in any way comparable with that of the Skye ridge. There is plenty of rock climbing. Access to Rum has always been re-stricted—for many years it was kept strictly private by the owners and now it has become a Nature Reserve.

The Cuillin Hills of Skye, near the south end of the island, and without doubt Britain's finest mountains, take the form of a continuous ridge which never falls below 2,500 feet throughout its 15-mile length. The peaks are of gabbro, a wonderfully rough rock of dark grey or even purple colour, and carry little vegetation but many midges; the inter-linking ridges are narrow and wall-like. The southernmost hill is Gars Bheinn above Loch Scavaig and from here the ridge runs north-west-wards for three miles to Sgurr na Banachdich (3,167 feet), 'the small-pox peak' or perhaps 'peak of the milkmaid'. On the way the branch ridge of the Dubhs runs down eastwards towards Loch Coruisk, while soon after another on the opposite side links to Sgurr Alasdair (3,251 feet), the highest point of the range, beyond which on the spur called Sron na Ciche is the greatest of the local climbing crags. Coire Lagan lies between here and the main ridge, which continues over Sgurr Mhic Coinnich (3,107 feet) to Sgurr Dearg (3,206 feet) and the Innac-cessible Pinnacle. The latter is a horn of rock, the resistant remains of a dyke of trap rock, which, overtopping the summit of Sgurr Dearg by 20 feet, is thus the second highest mountain of the Cuillin. Beyond Sgurr na Banachdich the ridge turns north-eastwards for two miles over Sgurr a'Ghreadaidh (3,190 feet) and Sgurr a'Mhadaidh (3,010 feet), 'the foxes' peak' (pronounced 'Vatee', we are told), to Bidean Druim nan Ramh. From here a long subsidiary ridge runs parallel to the earlier part of the main ridge described above, and cradled between them is Coir-uisg with the famed Loch Coruisk. At An Caisteal the main ridge turns north for half a mile to Bruach na Frithe (3,143 feet), perhaps the easiest peak to climb and a fine viewpoint. The final section runs eastward for a further half-mile over the fantastically shaped Bhasteir Tooth to the fine triple ridged peak of Sgurr nan Gillean (3,167 feet), 'the peak of the young men', above Sligachan. All the above hills, known as the Black Cuillin, lie between Glen Brittle on the west and Glen Sligachan. On the far side of the latter two more peaks, Blaven and Clach Glas, are of gabbro and thus fall in the Black Cuillin, but the remainder are of pinkish granitic rocks, smoother and more rounded, and are known as the Red Cuillin. Marsco and Glamaig are the highest summits.

The traverse of the main ridge from end to end is, perhaps, the finest mountain expedition in Britain, involving a large amount of scrambling and, if the crest be followed all the way, at least four serious pieces of rock work. It was first done by L. G. Shadbolt and A. C. Maclaren in 1911 in something over 12 hours; this has been progressively reduced by subsequent traversers to around four and a half hours. When Blaven is also included, as was first done in 1939, the expedition is known as the 'Greater Traverse'.

The earliest mention of the Cuillin was in the writings of Donald Munro in 1549—'many grate hills, principally Cuilluelum', while a century later they figured on a map of Skye prepared by Timothy Pont. Martin Martin, who travelled through the Western Isles early in the eighteenth century, found the Cuillin much the same as we do today, in one respect anyway: 'The Quillin, which exceed any of these Hills in height, is said to be the cause of much Rain, by breaking the clouds that hover about it, which quickly after pour down in Rain upon the quarter on which the wind then blows.' Pennant and MacCulloch, who climbed Beinn na Caillich above Broadford during their tours, both contented themselves with this view of the higher mountains; Boswell noted the Cuillin in passing, 'a prodigious range of mountains capped with rocky pinnacles in a strange variety of shapes', but from Dr Johnson came nothing but generalizations. Sir Walter Scott visited Loch Coruisk to get local colour for 'The Lord of the Isles' and it was the publication of this work which finally attracted visitors in large numbers. The hills, he wrote in his diary: ' . . . seemed to consist of precipitous sheets of naked rock, down which torrents were leaping in a hundred lines of foam. The tops, apparently inaccessible to the human foot, were rent and split into the most tremendous pinnacles . . . '.

The Cuillin are unique among British hills in that we know who made the first ascents of most of the mountains. Many were done in the latter half of the nineteenth century, the last, Sgurr Coire an Lochain, by J. N. Collie, W. W. Naismith and party as recently as 1898. The story begins in 1836 when Professor Forbes, scientist and alpinist, visited Sligachan and succeeded in reaching the top of Sgurr nan

Gillean with Duncan MacIntyre, a local forester. They found, Forbes tells us, that 'the extreme roughness of the rocks rendered the ascent safe, when, with any other formation, it might have been considerably perilous. Indeed, I have never seen a rock so adapted for clambering'. He came back in 1845, climbing Bruach na Frithe and Sgurr nan Gillean again, and afterwards made a map and wrote an account of the geology. During the next 25 years Blaven, Sgurr na Stri and Sgurr a' Ghreadaidh were climbed by various visitors, the party on the last including John Mackenzie, who in later years became famous as the local mountain guide. In 1865 Sheriff Alexander Nicolson, born in Skye and by turns writer, journalist and lawyer, began spending exploratory holidays among the mountains of his birthplace. He climbed Sgurr nan Gillean, descending by a new way, a cleft still called 'Nicolson's Chimney'. 'Down which', he tells us, 'the only mode of progression was crawling on our backs. During the last few yards of this vermicular descent we could not see where we were to step, and great was my satisfaction when I found my heels resting at the foot of the precipice among a heap of debris'. In 1873 he reached the summit of the highest point of the range, then unnamed, subsequently called after him Sgurr Alasdair, while in the following year he added Sgurr Dubh Mor to his conquests.

Alpine climbers were by now coming on the scene in increasing numbers and most of the remaining summits fell within the next few years. The Pilkington Brothers were particularly active with, in 1880, the Inaccessible Pinnacle and, in 1887, Sgurr Mhic Coinnich (named after John Mackenzie) and Sgurr Thearlaich (named after Charles Pilkington). J. Norman Collie was another famous climber closely associated with these mountains throughout his climbing career. Except for Sgurr Coire an Lochain he arrived too late for first ascents of summits, but he was responsible for many of the easier rock climbs including the Thearlaich–Dubh Gap, the Bhasteir Tooth and the famous pinnacle called the Cioch, which juts out from the crag of Sron na Ciche. Collie began climbing during a fishing trip to Skye in 1886 and thereafter the Cuillin became part of his life; in due course he too had a peak named after him—Sgurr Thormaid, on the Ridge between a'Ghreadaidh and na Banachdich. He finally retired to Sligachan where he died in 1942:

The individuality of the Cuillin is not seen in their summits, which are often almost ugly, but in the colour of the rocks, the atmospheric effects, the relative largeness and harmony of the details compared with the actual size of the mountains, and most of all in the mountain mystery that wraps them round; not the mystery of clearness, such as is seen in the Alps and Himalayas, where range after range recedes into the infinite distance till the white snow peaks cannot be distinguished from the clouds, but in the obscure and secret beauty born of the mists, the rain, and the sunshine in a quiet and untroubled land, no longer vexed by the more rude and violent manifestations of the active powers of nature.

The Cuillin became the Mecca of British climbing, visited even by climbers from the south of England for whom the Alps were no farther distant. Ashley Abraham came and a weighty *Rock Climbing in Skye* followed, reflecting the simple joys of the climbing scene half a century ago:

> Poised upon the ridge are some loose blocks. These are crossed, and then the Policeman bars the way. He is only orthodox in his methods in that he regulates the traffic to a nicety. A fine sense of discrimination is his. His policy is not that of 'Move on', but one of 'Move off'. Like some of his human namesakes, he is mostly bluff, however, and if dealt with in the proper way, proves amenable to reason. You must keep on the right side of him. The holds are upon that side. The wind is generally upon the other, and tends to blow one off. The climber hugs him as closely as though he were a human being and the climber a vagrant after a club dinner. With his arms round the neck of the Policeman, he reaches home, or, rather, the easier part beyond.

The waves of intensive exploration which washed over the high crags of England and Wales hardly reached here and experts from the south seemed content to enjoy the hills and the routes without worrying about the untouched rocks around them. It was not until after World War II, when large numbers of Scots took a hand, that standards began to approach those of the mainland mountains and accounts to take on the familiar language of terse understatement, as in this excerpt from an account of a new climb by Tom Patey:

> Below the piton, traverse 20 feet to the right on good holds and climb 10 feet to a precarious lodgement at the foot of a fierce holdless diedre. Scattered holds for 25 feet lead to the start of the thin section, where a

security piton was left in place—it is poorly placed for direct aid (for which it is not intended). Very tenuous for 20 feet above the piton, to a rehabilitation foothold; then the diedre relents. Piton belay . . .

The northern peninsula of Skye, Trotternish, is also hilly. The Storr (2,360 feet) rises six miles north of Portree and among several pinnacles on its eastern flanks is the Old Man of Storr, some 160 feet high and only recently climbed. These basalt hills continue northwards to Meall nan Suireamach (1,779 feet), below which the Needle Rock in the Quirang is 100 feet high and unclimbed. The island of Raasay faces Trotternish across a narrow sea channel. The highest point here is Dun Caan (1,456 feet) where Boswell is said to have danced a jig in 1773. To the south Scalpay reaches 1,298 feet.

*   *   *   *   *

The Outer Hebrides, also called the Long Island, stretching from Barra Head to the Butt of Lewis, are some 15 miles west of Skye. A number of the islands are mountainous, while others are unusually flat. In the south Barra reaches 1,260 feet at Heaval. The next major island, as we move northwards, is South Uist, the main hills of which, towards the north end, are of gneiss (Bheinn Mhor, 2,034 feet). Benbecula, the next, is described as a 'maze of land and water' and the summit is a mere 409 feet. North Uist is similar though the highest hill, Eaval, is 1,138 feet. This, the guidebook tells us, 'is almost completely surrounded by water . . . in this boggy, trackless, flat and maze-like area, a map and compass would seem a *sine qua non*, at least for one who hoped to return'. North Uist has the lowest 'ben' in Scotland—Bheinn a Bhaile, only 72 feet.

Lewis and Harris form one island, the largest and most mountainous in the Outer Isles. The chief hills are in North Harris and are of gneiss. This forms many fine crags suitable for climbing, though difficulties of access have so far saved them from exploitation on a large scale. Clisham (2,622 feet), the highest hill, is four miles north of Tarbert and from it the hills run westwards to the sea with several more 2,000-foot peaks. The outstanding crag is the overhanging Strone Ulladale, the 800-foot rock face of which overhangs the base by many yards. Farther north the Uig hills in Lewis rise to 1,885 feet at Mealisval; there are some fine crags here also, notably Creag Dhubh Dhibadail on Tamanaisval, said by one party to be 'the most unrelenting wall of rock that we have seen anywhere'. In the district of Park in east Lewis Beinn Mhor is 1,874 feet, while in north Lewis the lower hills are diversified by some fine antiquarian remains, such as the standing stones at Callernish— 'next in importance to Stonehenge'.

The islands of St Kilda lie some 50 miles west of Harris. From Conachair (1,397 feet) on the main island of Hirta steep cliffs drop almost vertically into the sea. Soay to the north-west, which gives its name to a well-known breed of mountain sheep, has cliffs all round and some climbing is needed to reach the summit (1,114 feet). In the strait between these islands is Stac a'Biorrach (236 feet), a famous climb. The island of Boreray is four miles north-east of Hirta and close to it are two more huge stacks, Stac an Armin (592 feet), where the last of the Great Auks was killed in 1840 and Stac Lee (533 feet), which has been described as 'the most majestic sea rock in existence'. Long before rock climbing emerged as a sport the islanders used to climb these cliffs and stacks to collect sea-birds' eggs and climbing ability became a decisive asset for a prospective husband. Rockall, way beyond St Kilda, though only 70 feet high, may perhaps be regarded as a mountain summit, for in between the bed of the Atlantic falls away more than 1,000 fathoms.

The Orkneys, less than ten miles north of John o' Groats, are of Old Red Sandstone. The highest point is Ward Hill (1,565 feet) in the island of Hoy. St John's Head on the same wild island is the biggest vertical sea-cliff in Britain—1,141 feet. The Shetlands, 50 miles farther on, reach 1,475 feet at Ronas Hill on Mainland and 1,373 feet at Sneug on Foula. There are huge sea-cliffs and many different rock types. Here, the farthest north of the British Isles, there is no nightfall during summer months and hill and cliff expeditions can be prolonged at will with no fear of benightment. The aurora borealis is often seen, for we are now in the same latitude as Bergen, 225 miles to the east. Land's End lies nearly 800 miles behind; the Arctic Circle is only 300 miles ahead.

INDEX

The numerals in **bold type** refer to the **figure numbers** of the illustrations
Quoted Authors and Works are printed in italics

INDEX